D1084070

Science and International Affairs
Melvyn B. Nathanson, *General Editor*

RICHARD POLLAK

UP
AGAINST
APARTHEID

The Role and the Plight
of the Press in South Africa

Southern Illinois University Press
Carbondale and Edwardsville

Printed in the United States of America
Edited by Teresa White
Designed by Quentin Fiore

Production supervised by Richard Neal

Library of Congress Cataloging in Publication Data

Pollak, Richard.
  Up against apartheid.

  Includes bibliographical references and index.
  1. Government and the press—South Africa.
2. South African newspapers.   3. English newspapers—
South Africa. I. Title.
PN4748.S58P6   079'.68   80-22363
ISBN 0-8093-1013-9

Contents

Acknowledgments

Many journalists in South Africa helped enormously with this book, some at considerable risk to themselves. To these courageous men and women, who should be an inspiration to their colleagues around the world, I dedicate these pages.

I also thank M. J. Rossant and the Twentieth Century Fund for their encouragement and support in this project, and Pamela Gilfond for patient editing that improved the manuscript on almost every page.

Grateful acknowledgment is made to the *Index on Censorship*, Copyright © Writers & Scholars International Ltd London 1978, for permission to reprint the poem, "What dreams and visions we clutched," by Don Mattera.

New York   RICHARD POLLAK
August 1980

UP
AGAINST
APARTHEID

Introduction

The relationship between press and government in South Africa was uneasy at best in the two decades after the Nationalists came to power in 1948. But by the mid-1970s, antagonism between the two forces had become almost palpable as the Afrikaner regime hunkered down in defense of the besieged *Vaderland* and its political blueprint of apartheid. Outside the country, hostility came from almost every quarter. And the arrival of black leftist governments in neighboring Angola, Mozambique, and Zimbabwe did nothing to allay the Nationalists' growing sense of isolation. Within the nation the angry black majority became increasingly militant, never more so than on 16 June 1976 and in the weeks that followed. The uprising that convulsed the black ghetto of Soweto during that period was triggered by the government's insistence that black students learn Afrikaans, the language of their Afrikaner oppressors. But the uprising quickly grew to vent the whole range of frustrations felt by blacks, producing "race riots on a larger scale than has ever been experienced in South Africa."[1]

South Africa's newspapers reported these events in some detail, especially the English-language ones. As a result, they came into head-on collision with the government almost daily—not as in the United States, where generally polite sparring typifies media-government relations. (Watergate, as has been pointed out more than once, was a great exception to the genteel rule.) In South Africa a fury that sometimes borders on

1. *Survey of Race Relations in South Africa, 1976* (Johannesburg: South African Institute of Race Relations, 1977), p. 51.

I

mutual hatred characterizes the Nationalists and the English-language press. Out of this fierce brawl emerges the central argument of this book: that more than any powerful force in the country these newspapers stand almost alone between the Afrikaner government and totalitarian darkness.

Indisputably, other institutions and groups also oppose the Nationalist regime, some more vigorously—and radically—than the press. But if they were not weak when the Nationalists took over in 1948, they are now. After the general elections in November 1977, the official opposition in Parliament declined to 17 seats compared with the Nationalists' 134.[2] Judges still render justice occasionally, but after thirty years, the South African bench is by and large a respository of timid party hacks seldom willing to rule in the face of the government's repressive policies. Apartheid, and the apparatus of cruelty used to enforce it, have left the nonwhite majority in disarray—most of its leaders either cowed, exiled, imprisoned, or murdered by the state. Television could tell this sorry story vividly, but it is a one-channel propaganda machine operated by the government-controlled South African Broadcasting Corporation. Inside South Africa, newspapers serve as the lone megaphone of dissent. Without the still moderately free press to promulgate new and unpopular ideas, the country's political lopsidedness would be near complete.

Many enlightened South Africans fear that day is at hand already, among them Anthony Mathews, head of the law department at the University of Natal in Durban and one of the country's leading legal scholars. In his book comparing restraints on the free flow of information in the United States, Great Britain, and South Africa, Mathews writes of his own country: "The information which the press can get is limited and that which it can publish even more circumscribed. . . . Government's intervention is not limited to rigid controls, but nowadays includes instances of 1984-style remaking of knowledge and information."[3] Mathews does not hyperbolize. The

2. *South Africa '78: Official Yearbook of the Republic of South Africa*, 5th ed. (Pretoria: South African Bureau of National and International Communication, 1978), p. 188.

3. Anthony Mathews, *The Darker Reaches of Government* (Cape Town: Juta & Co., 1978), p. 172.

2

Orwellian manipulations he warns about were at the very heart of "Muldergate," the Department of Information scandal that rocked South Africa in the late 1970s and led to the downfall of Prime Minister B. J. Vorster.

The press's role in uncovering Muldergate proved its finest hour, and also its most difficult one, for the government came down with unprecedented ferocity in the wake of the newspapers' muckraking. To understand why—and to comprehend in general the unique context in which the press operates—a brief look at contemporary South Africa is essential.

South Africa's considerable natural endowments—a benign climate and a beautiful land rich in gold, diamonds, and other minerals—lie deep in the shadows of apartheid. As of mid-1977 the nation's estimated population totaled 26,923,000. Of this number, 19,361,000 were black (African), 2,432,000 colored (mixed race), and 765,000 Indian (Asian). The remaining 4,365,000 were white.[4] But despite their one-to-five minority, whites dominate every corner of South Africa's economy and politics. The nation's constitution denies the 22 million nonwhites the most basic civil rights, including the right to vote. Blacks may not own land or major businesses, their union activity is limited, and segregated education principally reinforces white supremacy. Apartheid laws proscribe everything from freedom of movement (blacks must carry identification passes when they travel or live outside their government-prescribed "homelands") to freedom to love (police may legally break into homes to apprehend interracial couples engaged in sexual intercourse).

Average white per capita income outstrips black income by eleven to one.[5] Blacks are free to purchase goods and services from whites, but to do so, they must face the daily insults of segregated toilets, restaurants, and buses, and the myriad other manifestations of "petty" apartheid. In Johannesburg, Cape Town, and a few other major cities, a token amount of integration now exists, largely as a public relations ploy. For example, in 1978 the government granted special status to 58 of the coun-

4. *South Africa '78*, p. 75.
5. *Survey of Race Relations in South Africa, 1978* (Johannesburg: South Africa Institute of Race Relations, 1979), p. 159.

try's 1,448 hotels.[6] "Many hoteliers reported that contradictions and anomalies in the restrictions . . . could cause difficulties with the guests," notes the *Survey of Race Relations in South Africa.* "Only black visitors holding foreign passports could use all hotel facilities. Other blacks could not drink in men's only bars. . . . They could swim if resident at the hotel, and be served liquor at mixed-sex bars if resident or a bona fide guest of a resident. Blacks who were not resident could be served liquor only if they were taking or about to take a meal on the premises, or attending a function, such as a conference."[7]

Since apartheid has become such a pejorative term worldwide, the government much prefers "separate development" or "plural relations." These euphemisms refer primarily to the homelands policy, by which ten territories throughout the country have been set aside for blacks—much as reservations were allotted Indians in the United States. South Africa covers 471,879 square miles, three times the size of California. The government has "given" 13 percent of this land to the blacks. Some of the homelands are fragmented into apartheid archipelagos. Bophuthatswana, for example, exists as seven separate land islands. Kwa-Zulu consists of no less than forty-four unconsolidated parcels. Most South African blacks are assigned to one of the ten homelands. The colored and Indian populations are not, in part because they do not pose nearly the numerical threat as the blacks, in part because most Nationalists are pigmentocrats and view the darker African as inherently more of a menace. The Nationalists justify the homelands policy with the argument that each major African language group needs its own territory in order to survive; moreover, the government maintains that "separate development" will permit blacks and whites to go forward together in peace.

Inevitably, this political abracadabra has failed—for the great Catch-22 of South African society is that no matter how determined the government is to stash blacks out of sight, the economic system rests on their cheap labor. In this highly industrialized and urbanized nation, that means blacks in the

6. Ibid., p. 364.
7. Ibid.

4

cities. Not just a few, but hundreds of thousands, rigidly segregated in teeming ghettos like the Southwestern Townships (Soweto), outside Johannesburg. According to 1977 estimates, the *de jure* population of the ten homelands was roughly 19 million. In fact, only 9,400,500 people actually resided in them[8]—a high proportion of them wives and children separated from their husbands and fathers, who live and work in the cities or at the mines. Eventually, all homelands are to become independent states. But even the Transkei, which on 26 October 1976 became the first to receive this status, cannot hold much more than half its *de jure* population of 4,032,000.[9] In short, the homelands, "independent" or not, essentially function as black labor reserves for a white government that has set aside 87 percent of South Africa for itself.[10]

The political struggle between the two principal white factions in South Africa is much less understood than the black-white collision. Some 60 percent of the country's 4.4 million whites are Afrikaners, descendants of the Dutch settlers who arrived at what is now Cape Town in the middle of the seventeenth century.[11] Most of the remaining whites descend from the British, who brought their imperialism to the bottom of Africa in the nineteenth century. The Afrikaners, or Boers, were essentially farmers, a simple people steeped in Calvinism and its fundamental interpretation of the Bible. The British, who sailed into Cape Town 160 years after the Dutch, were both cosmopolitan and condescending—in the latter case, often as much as the Afrikaner is to the black today.

For decades the British pushed the Boers around almost at will. In the 1830s the Boers fled this patronizing domination in a "Great Trek" north from Cape Town. Like American pioneers

8. *Survey, 1978*, p. 272.

9. Ibid.

10. So committed are the Nationalists to the homelands policy that they are officially shrinking their country. The area of 471,879 square miles generally accepted as the size of South Africa is given in the government's 1978 yearbook as 440,355, a reduction obtained by subtracting the area of the "independent" homelands of Transkei and Bophuthatswana. Similarly, an estimated 19 million blacks live within what the world considers South Africa's borders; yet the yearbook lists about 15 million because the government no longer counts the population of the two homelands.

11. *Encyclopaedia Britannica: Macropaedia*, 17:66.

opening the West, they traveled in wagons that they drew into circles *(laagers)* when attacked by African tribes. Out of this harsh life, they carved two republics of their own, the Transvaal and the Orange Free State. For a while Britain tolerated this arrangement. But once gold and diamonds were discovered in the Boer republics, a divided South Africa proved less and less palatable. The British tightened their economic stranglehold on the area. The Afrikaner farmers, with no place to go, finally fought back. The result was the Boer War (1899–1902), which Britain won decisively, devastating both Boer republics.

The reconstruction period that followed culminated in South Africa's entry into the British Commonwealth in 1910. Boer General Louis Botha became the first prime minister of the Union of South Africa. But for all the surface political harmony, the seeds of a fierce Afrikaner nationalism were sprouting—the fruit of years of second-class citizenship for the Afrikaner in his own country. During the two years before union, the minister of education in the Orange River Colony, Gen. James Barry Munnik Hertzog, angered the English-language press and its readers by insisting that both English and Afrikaans be taught and stressed equally in the schools. In 1912 he went much further, arguing in several public speeches that the Afrikaans and English cultures should flow in two distinct and separate streams. On 7 December 1912 in his speech at De Wildt, Cabinet Minister Hertzog declared that "In the event of a conflict of interests [with Great Britain] he would place the interests of South Africa first."[12] Botha demanded Hertzog's resignation, and when he refused to step down, the prime minister himself resigned and formed a new cabinet without him. But the march to full Afrikaner power had begun. On 1 July 1914 the Nationalist party, committed to independence from the British Empire, officially came into existence, with Hertzog the leader of its tiny band.

In the three and a half decades that followed, uneasy truces alternated with volatile upheavals in South African politics. But through it all, one trend remained constant: the steady advance of Afrikaner nationalism. After World War II, political liberals—mostly British—spoke of creating a more racially just

12. *South Africa '78*, p. 46.

society, and some cautious moves were made in that direction. But the Afrikaners quickly galvanized the Nationalist party and, united under the banner of apartheid, in 1948 gained control of Parliament for the first time. It was a narrow victory made possible in part by a system of rotten boroughs that weighted the voting in favor of the Afrikaner farmer. With every subsequent election, the Nationalists increased their hold on South African politics.

Over the years, South Africa's blacks sought to counter the Afrikaner political juggernaut, principally through two organizations: the African National Congress (ANC) and the Pan-Africanist Congress (PAC). The ANC, founded in 1912, was essentially a reformist party, similar to the National Association for the Advancement of Colored People or Martin Luther King, Jr.'s, Southern Christian Leadership Conference in the United States. The slowly emerging black professional class that made up the ANC leadership believed that South Africa's future lay in integration through cooperation with the country's white liberals. But the "Africanist" bloc within the ANC, which eventually broke away and formed the PAC in 1959, wanted no part of interracial partnership; on the contrary, its aim was to destroy both pillars of the white temple—Afrikaner and English—and substitute total black rule.

Predictably, the government saw little to distinguish between the threats of the ANC and PAC. In 1960 the Nationalists outlawed both organizations under the omnibus Suppression of Communism Act. The leaders of each organization—Nelson Mandela (ANC) and Robert Sobukwe (PAC)—were imprisoned as threats to internal security. Mandela remains incarcerated two decades later. Sobukwe was released from prison in April 1969 but was required to report daily to a police station until his death from cancer on 26 February 1978. The ANC and PAC have continued to operate out of neighboring African countries and elsewhere in the world.

Inside South Africa the vacuum created by the banning of Mandela and Sobukwe was filled in the mid-1970s by the Black Consciousness Movement (BCM). Under the articulate leadership of Steve Biko, the movement began to create a committed constituency, especially among the radical young. But on 12

7

September 1977 the thirty-one-year-old Biko died after twenty-six days in detention; he had been manacled, kept naked for days, and severely beaten.[13] The worldwide outcry over his death moved the government to crack down further. On October 19 it declared seventeen black consciousness organizations unlawful under the Internal Security Act (successor to the Suppression of Communism Act). Moreover, it banned Biko's staunch supporter and friend Donald Woods, editor of the *East London Daily Dispatch*. And it closed down the *World* and *Weekend World*, the country's largest black newspapers, at the same time detaining their editor, Percy Qoboza. By way of explanation, Minister of Justice James Kruger said that the banned publications and organizations had been used by "organizers" to foster a revolutionary atmosphere in the country.[14] In May 1979 seven of the seventeen organizations banned on 19 October 1977 pooled their resources to form one body: the Black Consciousness Movement of South Africa (BCMSA). Regional committees were set up in New York, London, Bonn, Zambia, Botswana, and Lesotho. The new organization seeks to unify all banned liberation groups, including the ANC and PAC.[15]

Though the bustling streets and clipped suburbs of Johannesburg exude a surface calm, a siege mentality rules South Africa today. Neighboring Mozambique and Angola have been leftist black-ruled nations since wresting their independence from Portugal in 1975. Rhodesia became Zimbabwe in 1980, also with a left-wing, black-dominated government. In the United Nations, black Africa calls repeatedly for economic sanctions. On U.S. campuses, students and faculty clamor for withdrawal of American investment in South Africa. From Cape Town north through the Transvaal, guerrillas hector the government, hoping to ignite the revolutionary spark that will lead to black majority rule. In the urban townships, protests, riots, and sabotage increase as young blacks grow more radical and militant daily. And as always for the Afrikaner, the specter of communism looms everywhere.

13. *Survey of Race Relations in South Africa, 1977* (Johannesburg: South Africa Institute of Race Relations, 1978), pp. 159–64.

14. Ibid., p. 168.

15. *Transvaal Post*, 10 June 1979.

In this climate of paranoia and fear, the only *major* antigovernment force still operating is the English-language newspapers. In general, they echo (and amplify) the liberal political views of their British kinsmen in the Progressive Federal party (PFP), the hopelessly outgunned opposition in Parliament. With varying intensity over more than three decades, this press has consistently opposed apartheid, arguing that the white minority must face up to South Africa's racial arithmetic. On just how to do this, the English-language press has been a good deal less clear. Britain's nineteenth-century imperialism left South Africa's English community with a huge economic stake in the country. The Afrikaner may control the government, but the English establishment controls the economy. English money also controls the English-language press. Consequently, the newspapers are disinclined to offer political programs that might jeopardize their patrons' financial hegemony. Since an end to apartheid would mean granting full political rights to the overwhelming nonwhite majority, editorials in the English-language press tend to beat around the thorny bush. Nonetheless, the role of the English-language press is critical because it provides a highly visible forum for information and ideas inside South Africa and because its reporting has been relayed around the world by a corps of sympathetic foreign correspondents.

Although allowed to operate, the English-language press has met continuous opposition from the Nationalists. At the relatively benign end of the scale, press cards are arbitrarily denied certain reporters by the police, and every few years the government threatens to legislate a statutory press council and code, thus "persuading" the newspapers to do their own "voluntary" policing. At the numbing end are the bannings, detentions, and torture of journalists under a growing labyrinth of draconian laws proscribing freedom of the press.

Louis Le Grange, minister of Public Works and Tourism, stated the Afrikaner case baldly to a gathering of South African newspaper proprietors in October 1978. It had been a year since the government had banned Donald Woods and detained Percy Qoboza. But in case the owners had forgotten the crackdown, Le Grange reminded them that freedom of the press was not a right but a privilege granted by the government.[16] Journalists across the country reacted with dismay; but like all such periodic messages, it got across.

16. *Durban Tribune,* 22 October 1978.

2 The Other Separate Development, British v. Afrikaner

The press of any nation inevitably is a product of the historical and political forces it covers. But in few countries is this development so starkly apparent as in South Africa. Founding of the first newspaper in 1824, the *South African Commercial Advertiser* in Cape Town, launched a tradition of the newspaper as house organ for the competing white political points of view. Though race dominates the headlines today, as it does the country, the issue is of relatively recent vintage. Before the Nationalists embarked on the road to apartheid in 1948, newspapers in both English and Afrikaner camps preoccupied themselves with their own game of separate development.

The English-language press served primarily as a mouthpiece for the British capitalist. The now giant Argus Printing and Publishing Company, formed at Cape Town in 1866, was controlled by mining interests. So, too, were the *Diggers News,* the *Mining Argus,* and the *Standard and Transvaal Mining Chronicle,* which began publication with the opening of the Witwatersrand gold fields and the founding of Johannesburg in 1886. The *Rand Daily Mail* also received its major impetus from a mining baron, Sir Abe Bailey, who acquired the paper in 1905, three years after its founding.

The giant mining companies still wield considerable power in the press. Uni Rhodes Mining and Finance Ltd., for example, owned almost 13 percent of South African Associated Newspapers (SAAN) in 1978. Johannesburg Consolidated Investment Co. Ltd., another mining conglomerate, owned 250,000 shares of Argus.[1] As of 1978 Argus owned 39 percent of SAAN, and SAAN owned almost 7 percent of Argus.[2] Argus director P. H. Anderson is a former president and vice-president of the Chamber of Mines and a former managing director and chairman of Rand Mines Ltd.[3] The chairman of the Argus board, L. E. A. Slater, is also a director of SAAN—and chairman of the Central News Agency, the near monopoly distribution company owned heavily by Argus.[4]

Not only have the English-language newspapers carried the colors of industry, but for some fifty years they had the newspaper field to themselves. The first Afrikaner newspaper—*Di Afrikaanse Patriot*, published at Cape Town—did not appear until 1876. It, too, represented a special interest: the First Afrikaans Language Movement, "generally regarded as the midwife for Afrikaans as a written language."[5] In the years that followed, the Afrikaans-language press developed almost exclusively to promote Afrikaans and to preserve the Afrikaner culture against the pervasive British influence. But by 1915, a year after the Nationalist party was formed, the Afrikaans-language press had turned toward overt political nationalism. In the first issue of the Afrikaners' first daily—*De* (now *Die*) *Burger*, in Cape Town—editor D. F. Malan stated that "We recognize the existence of an Afrikaner nationalism with which we are in accord, and of which we hope to be a representative and interpreter." Sixty-three years later, not much has changed. As former *Die Burger* editor P. J. Cillie put it, "I've told my friends in the English press that I'm not going to fight against my political colleagues for them. We support the Nationalist Party. We criticize it, but to make it better. By and large, its battles are our battles."[6]

A strong cross-pollination characterizes Afrikaner jour-

---

1. *Who Owns What on the Johannesburg Stock Exchange* (Johannesburg: Financial Analysis, 1978), n. pag.

2. Ibid.

3. *Who's Who in South Africa* (Johannesburg: Argus Printing and Publishing Co., 1979), p. 89.

4. Ibid., p. 539.

5. *South Africa '78: Official Yearbook of the Republic of South Africa*, 5th ed. (Pretoria: Bureau of National and International Communications, 1978), p. 790.

6. Interview with P. J. Cillie, Cape Town, 30 October 1978.

nalism and politics. *Die Burger* editor D. F. Malan led the Nationalist party to power and served as prime minister from 1948 to 1954. H. F. Verwoerd, the builder of apartheid who became prime minister in 1958, began his career as the first editor of *Die Transvaler*, the Transvaal equivalent of *Die Burger*. While prime minister, Verwoerd assumed chairmanship of the company that ran the daily—as did B. J. Vorster when he became prime minister after Verwoerd's assassination in 1966. When P. W. Botha became prime minister, in 1978, *Die Burger* announced that "It has a special meaning for us because for many years he was closely connected with *Die Burger*, among other things as a director of the [paper's holding company]." Unlike his predecessors, Botha resigned from the holding company when he took office—and soon afterward urged others to do likewise. At the time, at least ten high-ranking Nationalist politicians served on the boards of either the Transvaal-based Perskor or the Cape-based Nasionale Pers, the two Afrikaner newspaper conglomerates.

This lockstep relationship between the Nationalist party and its press keeps much of the latter afloat. In both circulation and advertising, the English-language papers do much better than their Afrikaner competitors. In Johannesburg, for example, the *Mail*'s circulation (129,068) is double that of *Beeld* (63,032), its rival in the morning field. In the afternoon, the *Star* (170,242) outstrips by almost 24,000 the combined circulation of *Die Transvaler* (82,169) and *Die Vaderland* (64,389). Only the nationally distributed weekend papers compete fairly evenly: the *Sunday Times* (465,074), *Rapport* (403,493).[7] To counterbalance the English newspapers' financial superiority, the government indirectly subsidizes the Afrikaans-language press: by granting it printing contracts for everything from telephone books to school texts. Technically, such assignments are decided by competitive bidding, which often takes place, but Perskor or Nasionale Pers almost always win. Perskor also prints—in both English and Afrikaans—*Family Radio & TV*, the weekly magazine of program listings published by the state-run South Africa Broadcasting Corporation.

7. All figures represent average net sales for July–December 1978 and are compiled by the Audit Bureau of Circulations of South Africa Ltd.

As in almost all other industrialized nations today, monopoly rules South African journalism. Virtually all the major newspapers in the country are now published by one of four conglomerates: Argus, SAAN, Nasionale Pers, or Perskor. Argus, with a significant minority interest in SAAN, twice tried to take SAAN over (1968 and 1973), but was thwarted each time.

Despite conglomeration, many South African newspapers operate near the red or as outright money-losers. As a group, Argus is indisputably healthy, its Johannesburg *Star* and *Cape Argus* way out front in circulation and fat with ads. But most Afrikaans-language dailies could not survive without the protective umbrella of their holding companies—and the government contracts that buttress them. And more than one SAAN paper is financially wobbly, too, including the *Rand Daily Mail.* In February 1978 the paper laid off some two dozen editorial employees, cutting the staff by 25 percent. The financial precariousness of South African journalism owes primarily to an overabundance of newspapers. For example, Johannesburg, the country's largest city with a population of roughly 1.5 million, simply cannot support all ten daily and Sunday papers that circulate there.

This condition inevitably leads to a fierce competition for readers. And one result is that most newspapers—English and Afrikaans alike—reflect some of the worst excesses of British popular journalism. Screaming headlines, played-up crime news, and plenty of cheesecake are indispensable daily ingredients. "We've got a very nice bird sitting on top of a car," said the *Mail*'s Benjamin Pogrund during a discussion of Motorama coverage with his staff. "Let's try and run a color picture of her tomorrow."[8] And the paper did. Much of the Afrikaans-language press now eagerly bird-watches, too, in prurient defiance of its readers' Calvinist upbringing. "A nice woman in a bathing costume is a good thing, but the picture must be tasteful," says *Die Burger*'s Cillie. "You can have almost complete nakedness so long as it is there not to shock but to please."[9] South African editors and reporters feel the overall quality of their newspapers has declined measurably in recent years. "It's

8. *Rand Daily Mail* editorial meeting, Johannesburg, 24 October 1978.
9. Interview with P. J. Cillie, Cape Town, 30 October 1978.

very difficult to build up morale these days," says Martin Schneider, the *Mail*'s political reporter.[10]

Schneider is white. Black journalists in South Africa feel even more discouraged. "We don't have a single truly black paper in this country," says Zwelakhe Sisulu, formerly one of Schneider's colleagues on the *Mail*. "*The World* was heading in that direction in spite of itself. The [1976] Soweto uprising determined the course the paper would take. There is no black editor who could ignore those events and still live in Soweto. There was immense pressure on the black establishment in the township."[11] Sisulu and most other black journalists regard the chances of establishing an independent black press as absolutely nil, a view hardly dispelled by the shutdown of the *World*. To Pretoria, Percy Qoboza and his paper posed an enormous threat: a black-edited paper with a growing reach into just the communities the government wants to keep tamped down. "There is a huge market for a mass circulation black paper," says *Cape Times* editor Anthony Heard. "There was always a very good chance *The World* would be banned because of its power potential."[12]

To many black journalists, however, this potential is largely an illusion: like the rest of their lives, ultimately it is governed entirely by whites. The *World* (and the *Durban Post* that expanded to replace it after the banning) is owned by the Argus Company, as is the *Cape Herald*, the weekly that circulates to the colored community in that province. In addition, Argus publishes *Ilanga*, a biweekly in Zulu distributed in Natal. Perskor puts out two publications for blacks, the weekly *Imvo*, in Xhosa and English, and the monthly *Bona*, in Zulu, Tswana, Xhosa, and Sotho. The only other periodical edited specifically for nonwhites is *Drum*, published fortnightly by Jim Bailey (son of *Rand Daily Mail* builder Abe Bailey) and printed by a subsidiary of Perskor. Even if the black community somehow managed to get up the considerable capital necessary to start its own paper, the project would be stymied: not just by the likelihood that the government would close it down, but by the fact that

10. Interview with Martin Schneider, Johannesburg, 25 October 1978.
11. Interview with Zwelakhe Sisulu, Johannesburg, 1 November 1978.
12. Interview with Anthony Heard, Cape Town, 31 October 1978.

South African law makes it impossible for blacks to own anything more substantial than the mom-and-pop stores that dot the townships.

Without a press of their own, nonwhite readers have increasingly supported the English-language press. In 1962 about 33 percent of daily readership was nonwhite. By 1977 nonwhite readership had climbed to 45 percent. Significantly, in that fifteen-year period, claimed readership for whites rose only 30 percent, compared to an increase of 80 percent for Asians, 125 percent for coloreds, and 250 percent for blacks.[13] According to a 1978 study, "In Cape Town, more coloreds than whites read the English papers; in Durban, Indian readers almost equal white ones. In Johannesburg, more blacks read the *Star*, *Rand Daily Mail*, and the *Citizen*, taken together, than whites. Including the huge black readership of the daily *Post*, blacks now outnumber white readers of Johannesburg's four English-language dailies by two to one."[14]

Though the antiapartheid message of the English-language press is undeniably genuine, the boost it gives circulation is not an uncalculated side effect. To increase readership, many papers also publish so-called extras, special sections that cater to—or, in the minds of many, patronize—nonwhites. These pages generally read like the *National Enquirer*. Typical was the *Sunday Times* Durban extra of 29 October 1978, which devoted most of page one to "Herbalist Made Man's Life Hell," "The Helpless Horror of Fatal Blaze," and "Attacked Clerk Sees Friend Hacked Up by Panga Mob." Much of the remaining space revealed nineteen-year-old Pam Corker, a local beauty contest aspirant, in a red bathing suit that plunged almost as deep as the ten-inch photograph. Like most nonwhite journalists, Norman West, a colored reporter for the *Sunday Times* in the Cape, has nothing but contempt for the extras. "We are guilty of speaking with a forked tongue," he says. "We preach one thing in our editorials but practice the opposite. We are perpetuating the apartheid policy of the government."[15] Most

13. C. A. Gifford, "Media Trends in South Africa" (paper delivered at a national conference, The Road Ahead, Grahamstown, South Africa, 7 July 1978).

14. William A. Hachten, "Black Journalists under Apartheid," *Index on Censorship*, May–June 1979, pp. 43–48.

15. Interview with Norman West, Cape Town, 30 October 1978.

nonwhite readers do not like the extras, either. "They confront us on them all the time," says Willie de Klerk, a colored photographer well known in the Cape for his work in the *Times* and *Argus* over the years. On one occasion nonwhite officials told him he could not take pictures at a track meet because they would appear in an extra.[16] Partly because of this hostility, both the *Cape Times* and the *Cape Argus* dropped their extras after a few years—with no appreciable effect on circulation. "As far as possible, we try to treat news on its merits," says John R. Coleman, senior assistant editor of the *Argus*. "But it's impossible not to have regard for politics. We have no doubt that our readers don't like too much 'black' news. At certain times one looks with envy on the kind of readership *Die Burger*'s got."[17]

This not-so-subtle racism permeates the newsrooms of all English-language papers, no matter how tough their antiapartheid coverage and editorials. For example, in the mid-1970s, a nonwhite reporter with ten years' experience earned about $464 a month—$232 less than a white reporter with comparable service. At the *Cape Times,* an assistant news editor and eight others on the twenty-five-member editorial staff are either black or colored. This is one of the better hiring records in South African journalism. But editor Heard fully concedes the paper "hasn't got on top of the recruiting problem." The *Times* takes on two nonwhite journalists a year, and after an eighteen-month training stint they join the full-time staff—"if they cut the mustard." (Statistically, these ratios compare favorably with nonwhite recruitment in U.S. newspapers—but only if the size of South Africa's nonwhite majority is ignored.) Candidates are sought out mainly in the schools and universities. But, says Heard, "black education is so bad that it is hard to find people up to our standards. Plus, any bright, young black tends to be politically embittered, and that causes trouble." Moreover, he adds, "the real crunch in South Africa comes when you put a black in charge of whites."[18] Very few blacks hold key management positions on white papers—even at the liberal SAAN, where roughly one quarter of the Johannesburg

16. Interview with Willie de Klerk, Cape Town, 30 October 1978.
17. Interview with John R. Coleman, Cape Town, 31 October 1978.
18. Interview with Anthony Heard, Cape Town, 31 October 1978.

employees on the *Financial Mail, Sunday Times, Sunday Express,* and *Rand Daily Mail* are black.

Forced into second-class roles, many nonwhite journalists long ago took on a carapace of cynicism. "I know from personal experience," says Zwelakhe Sisulu, "that stories from Soweto often never see the light of day. The editors tell me: 'We are reluctant to use this story; we don't want to meet the same fate as *The World.*' Once a newspaper is intimidated like that it has abandoned its ideals." To Sisulu and other nonwhite journalists, the newspapers' disclosure of the Muldergate scandal is a side issue to the true corruption in South Africa: apartheid. Sisulu argues that in chasing after Muldergate "the English-language press gives the government credibility. They can say, 'Look at the free press we have, look at how we are criticized.' "[19] In fact, government officials say exactly that. "We enjoy a helluva lot of freedom of the press here," says Vlok Delport, one of the government's chief information officers. "We have no reason to complain, especially compared to the rest of the world."[20]

Delport's statement typifies the Afrikaner's view of the press. He sees himself unfairly picked on in a world where dozens of nations hold their newspapers far more captive than South Africa. The citizens of Cape Town and Johannesburg, of whatever color, receive much more information about themselves and the rest of the world than their counterparts in Moscow, Peking, and the rest of the Communist bloc. In Latin America the press rarely gets as critical of the government as the English-language newspapers in South Africa. And most significant, in the Afrikaner's defensive view, a free press is virtually unknown in black Africa. Many whites advance this argument with unalloyed passion, as if the shutdown of the *World,* the detention of Percy Qoboza, and the constant harassment of journalists in general somehow become benign when considered in a worldwide perspective.

The sustained attacks of the English-language newspapers unquestionably infuriate the Nationalists. But their traditional commitment to a measure of *white* democracy—and the party's

19. Interview with Zwelakhe Sisulu, Johannesburg, 1 November 1978.
20. Interview with Vlok Delport, Pretoria, 26 October 1978.

concern for its image abroad—has so far served to keep the country's press relatively free. And few events illustrate this paradox more vividly than the pitched battle between the newspapers and the government over the scandal that came to be known as "Muldergate."

3 The Scandal Called "Muldergate"

On 8 May 1978 Prime Minister Vorster told Parliament that because of the "total onslaught" against South Africa "the government decided in 1972 to allocate funds to the Department of Information to assist it in a delicate and unconventional way in combatting . . . the subversion of our country's good image and stability."[1] Vorster put Cornelius P. Mulder in charge of the department, and when the minister took up the antisubversion challenge in 1972, he observed: "Information work, stated clearly and correctly, has also become security work for South Africa . . . the information officer is our frontline soldier."[2] Six years later, despite the deepening scandal that now sullied his stewardship, Mulder still talked tough: "we have, between 1972 and the present, created an apparatus . . . which can take up the cudgels for South Africa . . . when the survival of South Africa is at stake, no rules apply."[3]

Certainly this attitude prevailed in "Muldergate," the information scandal that embroiled South Africa throughout much of 1978 and 1979. No political upheaval in more than three decades of Nationalist supremacy so shocked the nation. Millions of rands in public funds had been appropriated and spent secretly for dozens of clandestine projects, ranging from the establishment of a progovernment daily in Johannesburg to an attempted purchase of the *Washington Star*, and possibly even

1. Republic of South Africa, *House of Assembly Debates* (Pretoria: Government Printer, 1978), 9 May 1978, cols. 6483–84 (hereafter cited as *Hansard*).
2. Ibid., 19 May 1972, col. 7712.
3. Ibid., 9 May 1978, cols. 6485–89.

The Scandal Called "Muldergate"

to a cover-up murder. Like Watergate in the United States, much of the information scandal initially surfaced in one newspaper—the *Rand Daily Mail.* Indeed, no voices irritate the Nationalists quite so much as those of the feisty *Mail* and its sister papers in the SAAN conglomerate. So in 1975 the government set out to secretly purchase the group with information department funds.

Late that year Gen. Hendrik Van den Bergh, head of the Bureau for State Security, flew to a cricket test match in the private jet of South African fertilizer magnate Louis Luyt. The general and Eschel Rhoodie, then secretary of the Department of Information and Mulder's right-hand man, told Luyt—as Luyt later testified—that they were in the process of taking over SAAN and "that they wanted to use me, especially my name and the fact that I was reasonably wealthy."[4] Luyt was also informed that Axel Springer, the West German publisher, and John McGoff, who runs a group of conservative papers in the United States, would be partners in the takeover.

Luyt, an up-from-poverty Afrikaner and supporter of the Nationalist party, pledged to buy more than $1 million in SAAN shares. And to add to the cover, Rhoodie drew an Afrikaner, Sir De Villiers Graaff, into the deal. Graaff, though long a leader of the political opposition, said he, too, could put up more than $1 million. How many others became involved, and for how much, remains unclear. But despite the bidders' willingness to pay a premium for the SAAN shares, their attempt failed. In early 1976 the stockholders closed ranks and a group of liberal backers established a trust designed to protect SAAN from future financial incursions from the right.

Even as the SAAN deal collapsed, the Department of Information had launched an ambitious contingency plan. If it could not buy up the opposition, at least it could counter with an English-language daily of its own. Thus, on 7 September 1976 the *Citizen* was born in Johannesburg. From the start, the morning tabloid took a slavishly progovernment line, and even before the start, charges abounded in the English-language press that the *Citizen* was secretly financed by the government, with Louis Luyt as front man. The allegation hung in the air for

4. *Rand Daily Mail,* 3 November 1978.

months, and for just as long, the Department of Information and the paper denied it. On 4 May 1978 the *Citizen* editorialized: "We dismiss with contempt the rotten smear by the Left-wing *Rand Daily Mail* about the finances of *The Citizen*." On May 10 in response to a question during a parliamentary debate over corruption in his ministry, Mulder stated that the Department of Information and the Government do not "give funds to *The Citizen*."[5] Even after the *Sunday Express*—SAAN's weekend tabloid in Johannesburg—flatly stated the opposite on 29 October 1978, the *Citizen* poured insults on the SAAN group and challenged the *Express* to prove its unequivocal report that the government had underwritten the *Citizen*.

Four days later, however, Judge Anton Mostert released a report on the Department of Information, and the *Citizen*'s guns fell silent. They could hardly have done otherwise. Mostert had been commissioned by the government to investigate foreign exchange irregularities; but what he uncovered about the information department proved far more explosive. In his testimony before Mostert, for example, Luyt confessed that he was Mulder and Rhoodie's front man in the *Citizen* scheme (codenamed Annemarie after Rhoodie's daughter). In explaining why he became involved, Luyt testified he was told that Vorster "had chosen me because I was not leftist or rightist—I was not in politics and I took a moderate line."[6] He also was a man used to dealing with large sums of money without attracting undue attention. In an agreement typed on Department of Information stationery and stamped "Most Secret," Rhoodie loaned Luyt $14 million to finance the *Citizen*. The conditions of the loan and the guidelines for the paper were laid out and signed under the terms of South Africa's stringent Official Secrets Act. The ground rules for editing the *Citizen* make its mission clear: "The paper shall undertake to publish nothing that will endanger the political, social or economic positions of the white population . . . shall not tolerate communism or further its aims . . . shall not undertake or publish anything that will endanger the constitutional chosen Government . . . [and] will at all times strive for the retention of the identity and their own political

5. *Hansard*, 10 May 1978, col. 6626.
6. *Rand Daily Mail*, 3 November 1978.

authority of the white population." The contract, signed by Rhoodie on 7 April 1976 on behalf of the Department of Information, also stipulated that the *Citizen* operate "on a healthy business basis with the intention of making a profit."[7]

The *Citizen* followed its editorial mandate to the letter, but the enterprise proved a financial disaster from the very beginning. "We calculated we could come through on the basis of interest on $14 million per year, and it was decided that $14 million would be advanced to me to invest," Luyt told Mostert.[8] The loan found its way to Luyt via a Swiss bank. With the full knowledge and approval of Mulder and Rhoodie, Luyt then placed the money in his own company, Triomf Kunsmis. There, it could produce 12.5 percent interest instead of eight or nine from a bank, Luyt told Mostert, adding: "After the loan, I got busy and found that the newspaper cost more than any of us ever dreamt—and the more we sold, the more expensive it became."[9]

To help meet the deficit, Luyt and the information department raised an additional $3.13 million in loans overseas. Luyt also sold half interest in his personal jet to a prominent Pretoria architect, Oscar Hurwitz, through an information department front organization called Thor Communicators. Hurwitz, a director of Thor and good friend of Rhoodie's, purchased the half share for $1.16 million on behalf of the department, which then dumped the money into the *Citizen* via Luyt. But the newspaper kept hemorrhaging. Moreover, Luyt and Rhoodie collided constantly over everything from the *Citizen*'s money woes to the information secretary's cavalier operating methods.

By February 1978 Luyt feared he might lose his estate because of the *Citizen*'s financial suction; reports circulated also that his once healthy company, Triomf, was in trouble and might even face bankruptcy. So the Department of Information arranged a sale that month to Hubert G. Jussen and J. Van Z. Alberts. Actually, transfer is a more accurate term, given that Jussen and Alberts were the founder and publisher of *To the Point*, a staunchly pro-Nationalist weekly "newsmagazine" also

7. Ibid.
8. Ibid.
9. Ibid.

secretly backed by the government. Alberts dreamed up the SAAN takeover idea, too, and is a close friend of Rhoodie's.

The *Citizen*'s new visible ownership also boasted two U.S. businessmen, a Dallas lawyer named David A. Witts and Beurt Ser Vaas, chairman of the Curtis Publishing Co. The company's flagship, the *Saturday Evening Post,* at one point listed only one foreign bureau on its masthead: Cape Town. In a March 1977 editorial on oil routes, the magazine stated: "Should the Cape of Good Hope fall into the sphere of the Soviets, American security will be threatened. When the lights of America go out, the world will indeed be dark." In the same issue, P. J. Cillie, the former editor of *Die Burger,* set down the case for the Afrikaner point of view. His article included a picture of South Africa's information minister and a caption that was both unintentionally prescient and ironic: "Connie Mulder—spoken of as the man most likely to one day succeed John Vorster. . . . His public views usually reflect official government policy on controversial issues."

But it was P. W. Botha who succeeded Vorster as prime minister in September 1978. When Mostert came to him on November 2 with the damning evidence against the Department of Information, Botha ordered the judge not to release it. The last thing the prime minister's new administration needed was judicial confirmation of all the English-language press had been hammering away at for months. But Mostert stood firm. Emerging furious from the meeting with Botha in Pretoria, he made the evidence public at a press conference and said: "I have endeavored to discover what particular interest of the state is furthered by suppression, albeit temporary, rather than disclosure of the evidence. I have been able to find none."[10]

The next day, November 3, the English-language dailies played up Mostert's revelations with unrestrained enthusiasm, none more so than the *Rand Daily Mail.* "It's all true!" declared the paper's page-one streamer headline in three-inch-high type. Along with the detailed reporting that began beneath it, an editorial observed: "Yesterday's disclosures came as a massive vindication of all this newspaper had published, and a repudiation of those who have tried to vilify the Rand Daily

10. Ibid.

Mail. We make no bones about it: we are proud of the role we have played. It was an even greater day for the judiciary. Every legal man should swell with pride at the courage Mr. Justice Mostert showed in resisting the Prime Minister's pressure to silence him."

For months, the Afrikaans-language newspapers either ignored the burgeoning Muldergate scandal or covered it with cautious follow-up stories. Now the major Afrikaans-language dailies began giving the story much more space. On November 3, for example, both *Beeld* and *Die Transvalar* ran mug shots of the principal actors in the unfolding drama across the top of page one. And *Beeld* warned in a page-one editorial that those responsible for the information scandal would have to pay. "Immediate withdrawal from public life will certainly not be enough," the paper stated, "but it is a first essential requirement."

Faced with the outcry that followed the Mostert revelations, an outcry now coming from inside as well as outside Nationalist ranks, Prime Minister Botha had little political choice but to initiate a new, fuller investigation into the scandal. So on the same day the newspapers exploded with the judge's findings, Botha handpicked a three-judge commission headed by Justice Rudolf P. B. Erasmus. The Erasmus commission delivered its findings to Parliament in three installments: the first at the beginning of December 1978, the second in March 1979, and the final one at the end of May 1979.[11] The Erasmus commission mostly confirmed the evidence given to Mostert and much of the newspaper coverage that preceded and followed it. But the reports reveal a good deal more as well and in terms of specifics occasionally prove riveting documents. For example, in the twenty-six months between the founding of the *Citizen* and establishment of the Erasmus commission, the paper spent state funds totaling $37 million.

Before dealing off the *Citizen* to Alberts et al., Secretary of

11. The Erasmus panel's formal title was Commission of Inquiry into Alleged Irregularities in the Former Department of Information. Its three reports were titled *Report* (December 1978), *Interim Report* (March 1979), and *Supplementary Report* (May 1979). All were published in Pretoria by the Government Printer, 1978 and 1979.

Information Rhoodie tried to persuade Michigan publisher John McGoff, his American friend, to buy the paper. McGoff had been involved as a potential investor in the attempt to purchase SAAN and, in general, is devoted to the Afrikaner cause. (McGoff also shared ownership of a game farm in the Eastern Transvaal with Mulder and Rhoodie.) After the government crackdown on the press and black militants on 19 October 1977, many U.S. media condemned the act. One notable exception was McGoff's newspapers, which offered a pro-Nationalist guest editorial by none other than J. Van Z. Alberts, publisher of *To the Point*. Ultimately, McGoff declined the *Citizen* setup. For one thing, he wanted control of the paper, and Mulder and Rhoodie were reluctant to give it up. For another, the deficit was running at an estimated $464,000 a month with no end in sight—a lot of money to funnel secretly from the Department of Information to McGoff, even by way of a Swiss way station. And perhaps, with the SAAN papers beginning to uncover the information scandal, McGoff feared he might get caught up in it.

As it turned out, he did anyway—for his attempt to purchase the *Washington Star* in 1974 and 1975 with the help of $10 million in Department of Information funds. McGoff insisted that his $25 million bid to take over the financially shaky *Star* contained not a dime of South African government money. But on 1 November 1978, below a page-one headline—"INFO'S U.S. PAPER BID"—the *Rand Daily Mail* categorically stated that Rhoodie sent McGoff the $10 million in early 1975 and that after the *Star* bid was rejected McGoff kept the money in his companies for two years.

Eventually McGoff spent $6 million of the $10 million to buy the *Sacramento Union* from the Copley chain and invested the remaining $4 million in running the paper. Moreover, in 1975 an additional $1,350,000 found its way to McGoff from the information department so he could buy a controlling share in United Press International Television News (UPITN), the second largest news-film producer and distributor in the world. According to testimony before the Erasmus commission, McGoff repaid $4,970,000 to the information department. In turn, Rhoodie reduced the balance of the loan to $1 million, thus writing off $5,380,000. In March 1978 the $1 million debt was sold to one of McGoff's partners for $30,000. Despite all the evidence gathered against him by the Erasmus commission and the press by mid-1979, McGoff steadfastly continued to deny he was Rhoodie and Mulder's South Africa connection in the United States. "I am not now, nor have I ever been," he said in July, "an agent or front for any foreign government, including the Republic of South Africa.[12]

According to the Erasmus commission, the Department of Information drew more than $74 million in secret government funds between 1973 and 1978. Much of this money came from the Department of Defense budget and then passed secretly through General van den Bergh's Bureau for State Security. P. W. Botha, minister of defense until becoming prime minister, objected to the arrangement; but Prime Minister Vorster liked Mulder's plans for, in the words of the commission, "projecting a true image of the RSA [Republic of South Africa] . . . countering hostile attacks from abroad; and even, if possible, swinging around world opinion in the Republic's favor."[13]

The *Citizen* accounted for approximately half the information department's $74 million pot. The remainder underwrote 160 to 180 secret projects. Consonant with the government's devotion to secrecy, the Erasmus commission concluded that it "is not expedient or even desirable to disclose" all the department's operating methods, "but examples must be mentioned to give some idea of the scope of the work."[14] Again, much of this information already had been covered by the press and the Mostert testimony. But the details provided by the Erasmus findings brought the whole picture into sharper focus.

A $957,000 interest-free loan to Afrikaner film producer Andre Pieterse now became crystal clear. Since 1970 Pieterse had been seeking to establish a black film industry in the country, one that would provide ideologically correct movies for black audiences. When Pieterse encountered difficulty raising money through conventional sources, he turned to his friend Rhoodie. An agreement was quickly struck, with Thor Com-

12. *Wall Street Journal,* 19 July 1979.
13. Commission, *Report,* chap. 2, par. 33.
14. Ibid.

27

municators, of which Pieterse was a director, fronting for the information department. Pieterse put together an expensive production staff for the project, but the government then shelved the idea. Meanwhile, Pieterse faced financial difficulties on *Golden Rendezvous,* an Alistair MacLean thriller he was translating to the screen. In January 1977 he persuaded Rhoodie to let him pledge the $957,000 as security for a production loan. Rhoodie agreed, but costs continued to mount, and finally, none of the major film companies would buy the rights. Ultimately, Pieterse used the $957,000 to pay off debts. (The *Rand Daily Mail* reveled in the Pieterse saga, running an advertisement for *Golden Rendezvous* on page one beneath a headline that announced: "Flop you paid for.")

The Department of Information also went into the real estate business at home and abroad. Between 1974 and 1978 it spent more than $1 million on fixed property, including a farm on which $27,840 was lost raising cattle. All this money flowed from an "emergency fund" set up within the secret fund against the day when cash might run short. The high-rolling Alberts, the department's most energetic front man, dipped into the emergency money to buy some flats in the Cape Town community of Clifton. Alberts' patron, Rhoodie, used the emergency fund to buy a plot at Plettenberg in Cape Province. The transaction involved several complex financial manipulations, ending on 16 September 1976. On that day, as the Erasmus commission puts it, "a telegraphic transfer of $51,800 from the Swiss Bank Corp." arrived in Rhoodie's personal account.[15] Judge Erasmus and his colleagues were anxious to discuss this particular deal with Rhoodie, but by the time they got around to examining it, he had fled the country.

Rhoodie made a specialty of travel. In January 1976 he ordered $7,000 paid from the secret fund to charter a jet that took a party of fourteen for sun and fun in the Seychelle Islands, a resort in the Indian Ocean popular with South Africans. A year later Rhoodie repeated the junket, this time sending the jet charter bill of $8,000 through Thor Communicators. Rhoodie and his wife were joined on both excursions by L. E. S. de

15. Ibid., chap. 8, par. 221.

Villiers and his wife.[16] Rhoodie, his brother, Deneys, and de Villiers constituted the information department's operating triumvirate. By 1978 one opposition M.P. was calling them "these Keystone Kops in the Marx Brothers Circus running around the world."[17] In one six-month period Deneys Rhoodie logged more than 200,000 miles in trips, including a flight from New York to Los Angeles ostensibly to check out "the services of a typist."[18] Standard government policy requires that official travel be booked through the state-run Railway Travel Bureau. But Rhoodie and his colleagues regularly used a private firm, aptly named Vacations Unlimited, which between 1973 and 1978 billed the department for $243,597.

Though underwritten by secret funds, very little of all this jetting about took place under much cover. Reacting to Rhoodie's Seychelles visits, H. H. Schwarz, the Progressive Federal party leader, observed: "It is so secret that the secretary (Rhoodie) starts off by sending a Telex message to . . . the Reef Hotel, in which he says: I am coming, and I am coming to see the President, so you must have a room for me . . . it is so secret . . . he is met by a Mercedes when he arrives at the airport and is given a banquet by the president. That is how secret it is."[19]

Another "secret" was the department's *hokkie,* a private box at the Loftus Versfeld rugby stadium in Pretoria. Rhoodie told Retief Van Rooyen, a Pretoria lawyer and the third director of Thor Communicators, that he needed the $4,640-a-year box to entertain important visitors. "I didn't want to sign the contract because the thing didn't look good to me," Van Rooyen told Mostert. "I couldn't see why the secret fund from information had to hire a public cubicle in front of 60,000 [people] at Loftus Versfeld."[20] But Van Rooyen went along nonetheless, with the money laundered through the bank account of his fellow director, film producer Pieterse. When the rugby season opened, a sign on the door of the secret *hokkie* announced: "Department of Information." The dismayed Van Rooyen

16. Ibid., chap. 6, pars. 158–59.
17. Ibid., 9 May 1978, col. 6469.
18. "A Watergate for Pretoria," *Time,* 13 November 1978, p. 52.
19. *Hansard,* 9 May 1978, col. 6470.
20. *Rand Daily Mail,* 3 November 1978.

suggested it hardly camouflaged the *hokkie,* so Rhoodie ordered the sign removed and substituted one reading, "Thor Communicators." Again, Van Rooyen protested; again, Rhoodie struck the sign, this time leaving the door blank. The *hokkie,* Van Rooyen by now had reluctantly concluded, "was for Dr. Rhoodie's family and friends."[21]

When not traveling or relaxing at rugby matches, Rhoodie and his colleagues presided over all manner of propaganda intrigue. They secretly underwrote, with more than $580,000, the supposedly independent, nongovernmental Southern African Freedom Foundation. Similarly, they established the Pretoria-based Foreign Affairs Association, an ostensibly private, quasi-academic group designed to convince officials overseas of South Africa's virtues. The department also secretly backed an Institute for the Study of Plural Societies, with Professor N. J. Rhoodie, also a brother of the secretary of information, as its head.

In the United States the department employed the New York public relations firm of Sidney S. Baron and Associates (at $603,000 a year) to promote South Africa. Former President Gerald Ford and Mulder addressed a gathering of high-level businessmen organized by Baron in Houston in June 1978. Security was so tight that even the U.S. State Department had trouble finding out who attended and what was said. "Neither Baron nor the South African embassy here in Washington would help," said one member of the South African desk. "They just told us to shove off."[22] In another attempt to influence the U.S. business community, several hundred dollars were given to Lester Kinsolving, the right-wing columnist, to buy stock in several major U.S. corporations, which allowed him to attend stockholders' meetings and counter antiapartheid groups. According to the Erasmus commission, the Department of Information eventually held shares in forty companies at home and abroad. The commission, maintaining the secrecy that still shrouds so much of the information scandal, does not identify the companies. On 7 December 1978 Prime Minister Botha told Parliament the government had evaluated 125 of the

21. Ibid.
22. Interview with U.S. State Department official who asked not to be identified, Washington, D.C., 15 December 1978.

department's secret projects. He announced that 57 would be scrapped. The remaining 68 operations would continue, 56 of them secretly.[23]

This penchant for cover-up characterized the scandal all along. Few scrambled quite so desperately as Information Minister Mulder. The popular leader of the Nationalist party's powerful Transvaal wing seemed Vorster's logical successor. But in 1978, with the election set for September, the information scandal broke all around him. When not denying the allegations outright, he maneuvered behind the scenes to save his political skin. In 1977 L. S. Reynders, a loyal Nationalist bureaucrat, had been appointed by Vorster to report on the alleged irregularities in the information department. But as it became clear that an honest disclosure would be ruinous politically, Vorster, Mulder, and General Van den Bergh forced Reynders to produce a whitewash. His "findings," exonerating the information department of any wrongdoing, were leaked to *Die Transvaler*, the official organ of the Nationlist party in the Transvaal, and were reported on 23 August 1978, about a month before the election. The leaker was Mulder, who also happened to be on the board of Perskor, the newspaper's parent company. Moreover, Mulder leaked only a portion of Reynder's brief report, leaving out what scintilla of skepticism it contained.

Initially, Reynders tried to justify his findings. But when pressed by the Erasmus commission, "he burst into tears and, like a lanced boil, made a clean breast of things."[24] He said he had produced the gloss under fierce pressure from Mulder and General van den Bergh, the former security chief who increasingly emerged as the shadowy manipulator behind much of the scandal. Reynders testified he even feared that if he opposed Van den Bergh, the general would "pulverize" him because "few people in this land realize what power Van den Bergh possesses."[25] The general did little to diminish this strongman image when he told the commission "that if he wanted to do something nobody would stop him and that he would stop at nothing."[26]

23. *Financial Times,* 8 December 1978.
24. Commission, *Report,* chap. 11, par. 383.
25. Ibid., chap. 11, par. 385.
26. Ibid., par. 386.

Including murder? Nine days before the November 30 general election in 1977 that gave the Nationalists their biggest majority, Robert and Jeanne-Cora Smit were fatally shot and stabbed at their home in Springs, a town east of Johannesburg. Smit was an Oxford-educated economist who had served as South Africa's delegate to the International Monetary Fund in Washington until 1975. More recently, he reportedly had uncovered widespread fraud involving government funds. He was about to become South Africa's finance minister and, according to close associates, planned to expose the guilty once in office.[27] Police first theorized that the Smits died in a ritual slaughter because of blood smears on the walls and the multiple stabbings that took place after each was shot; but subsequent clues indicated that perhaps a professional killer or killers had murdered the couple. No hard evidence linked the slayings to the Department of Information. But speculation persisted in both the English- and Afrikaans-language press. In late March 1979 Joseph F. Ludorf, a former South African justice, said he was counsel for a pilot who claimed to know how two West Germans, hired at $35,400 each to kill the Smits, were flown in and out of the country. Bits and pieces of the Smits' story appeared in the press, but serious investigation of the murders by journalists met classic Nationalist obstacles. On 21 November 1978, for example, Kitt Katzin, assistant editor of the *Sunday Express*, was ordered to appear in court to answer questions about a story he had written about the Smits' case.

At first glance, the political fallout from Muldergate would seem to presage dramatic change in South Africa. After all, as a result of the scandal, John Vorster, the country's prime minister for eleven years until he moved up to state president in 1978, resigned in disgrace on 4 June 1979. "For more than a year," the Erasmus commission concluded, "Mr. Vorster, together with Dr. Mulder, kept his knowledge of irregularities in the administration from his cabinet colleagues, at a time when the press and the opposition were already making insinuations and accusations against the Government."[28] Even before the commission issued its first report in December 1978, Mulder had

27. *New York Times*, 6 November 1978.
28. Commission, *Supplementary Report*, chap. 3, par. 60.

resigned, his political aspirations in tatters. The former information minister was also drummed out of the Nationalist party in April 1979, and the government ultimately charged him with contempt in August 1979 for refusing to give evidence before the Erasmus commission.

As for Rhoodie, after months on the lam in South America and Europe, he settled into high living on the French Riviera. There, in the resort town of Juan-Les-Pines, French police arrested him on 19 July 1979. Officially, the Nationalists wanted to extradite their former information secretary back so they could prosecute him for fraud. But as Rhoodie knew, his former colleagues and champions also were eager to shut him up. After bolting South Africa in November 1979, he claimed he dictated forty hours of incriminating recollections onto tapes. These he tried to peddle for $200,000 to the media around the world. When no takers stepped forward, he agreed to an interview with David Dimbleby of the British Broadcasting Corporation. On 21 March 1979 it took place at Rhoodie's undisclosed European hideaway. Rhoodie's performance was long on self-promotion and short on facts, but he promised that the latter— documents as well as tapes—were tucked away in two safes in a European bank. "I have made it clear already," he told Dimbleby, "that if I were to die an unnatural death cr if I were to be taken back to South Africa against my will or imprisoned on trumped-up charges and so on, then my lawyers have instructions what to do . . . the material would be released then."[29]

Elsewhere in the interview, Rhoodie served up tantalizing hints that a good deal might remain to be revealed about the information department's secret propaganda war. He suggested that South Africa had maneuvered behind the scenes to influence politics in Europe and America, that the department had been involved in helping to defeat two strong U.S. opponents of apartheid, Senators Dick Clark (D., Iowa) and John Tunney (D., California). Rhoodie implied that South African money had found its way into the coffers of groups eager to defeat the senators, such as the right-to-life organization that opposed Clark's proabortion position. One fact is clear: in early 1978

29. *Cape Times*, 22 March 1979.

33

Andrew Hatcher, a former John F. Kennedy press aide who is black and who moved on to work for Sidney Baron, promised Vorster that Clark would be defeated.

By the end of 1979 Rhoodie had yet to make good on his vow to reveal the damaging information he claimed to have collected on his former colleagues in the government. On 23 August 1979 he was extradited from France and taken under police guard to an undisclosed jail in South Africa. A month later, he was charged in Pretoria Supreme Court with fraud involving almost $100,000 in government funds. On October 8 the court sentenced him to six years in prison. His lawyer said he would appeal, and he was released on $108,000 bail on condition that he report to a police station daily and not leave the Pretoria-Johannesburg area. Meanwhile, Rhoodie's former boss and good friend, Cornelius P. Mulder, was getting much kinder treatment. On August 30, a week after Rhoodie was brought back from France, Mulder was acquitted of charges that he had obstructed the Erasmus inquiry into the information scandal. Mulder, too, had threatened to tell "the whole truth" if dealt with too harshly, and some government officials feared he might implicate Prime Minister Botha, who had been cleared of any involvement by the Erasmus commission.[30]

Despite all the investigation and subsequent political casualties of Muldergate, the scandal proved no victory for the *verligte* ("enlightened") Nationalists. On the contrary, it paved the way for Andries Treurnicht, who led the forces of *verkrampt* ("reactionary") Afrikaners decrying the stink of corruption that Vorster et al. had permitted to sully the party's Calvinist image. Treurnicht, a classically stern Boer right-winger, replaced Mulder as head of the party's Transvaal wing; by 14 June 1979 he had gathered sufficient strength to force Botha to take him into his cabinet as minister of public works.

On close inspection, the Erasmus commission findings do not emerge as particularly cleansing either. For all their revelations of high-level chicanery and castigation of official malfeasance, they are at bottom boosts for the status quo ante. In concluding its first report, for example, the commission recommended that the government legislate "a prohibition on the

30. *Washington Post*, 31 August 1979.

34

putting of questions to and the answering of questions by Ministers of Parliament if such questions relate to any Department's secret fund."[31] In its final installment, the commission criticized the Department of Information's secret funding of the Institute for the Study of Plural Societies. But it found the institute itself, which had been set up to give an intellectual patina to apartheid, "to have been productive since its inception and to have done good work on behalf of the RSA. . . . The Commission can find no good reason why its activities cannot be continued overtly instead of in secret as in the past."[32] Not a line in any of the commission's reports touches on the Smits' murders despite widespread speculation in the press that they were part of Muldergate. On the contrary, the commission accused the English-language press of hindering its investigation "by the publication of party-political propaganda stories."[33]

It is the supreme irony of Muldergate that P. W. Botha, who became prime minister only because Vorster's handpicked successor, Mulder, was buried under the avalanche of scandal headlines, should devote his first months in office to seeking revenge for the papers' "gossip-mongering."[34] On 11 December 1978, less than a week after the Erasmus commission weighed in with its first findings, Botha angrily vowed that when Parliament convened in 1979 the government would introduce yet more legislation aimed at muzzling the press.[35] He kept his word. By May, no less than five major press-curb bills were in the hopper at Cape Town. By far the most sinister, and cynical, was the Advocate-General Bill, a section of which prohibited publication of articles about public corruption and maladministration unless the information was first cleared by an advocate-general, a government investigation arm to be created by the legislation.

While waiting for Parliament to convene and consider the bills, the government hectored the press in other ways. At 2:30 A.M. on 12 March 1979, a court official telephoned the *Rand*

31. Commission, *Report*, chap. 14, par. 485.
32. Commission, *Supplementary Report*, chap. 5, pars. 66–67.
33. Ibid., chap. 2, par. 3.
34. *New York Times*, 12 December 1978.
35. Ibid.

Daily Mail and ordered the paper to kill several paragraphs in a story dealing with Minister of Justice J. M. Kruger's alleged involvement in an aspect of the information scandal. The final edition of that day's *Mail* ran with six inches of blank space on page one. That same night, the Erasmus commission sought to end further reporting of Rhoodie's European talkativeness by seeking injunctions against the *Mail* and the *Cape Times.* The week before, John Mattisonn, a political correspondent for the *Sunday Express,* was sentenced to fourteen days in jail for refusing to reveal the source of a Muldergate story he had written.

All three papers, of course, belonged to the South African Associated Newspapers group. Kitt Katzin of the *Express* and Mervyn Rees of the *Mail* did more to expose the information scandal than anyone else. Their colleagues in the more cautious Argus group played follow-up for months. The Afrikaans papers either ignored or dismissed the story for a long time, doubtless hoping it would somehow go away. But when it did not, reporting grew tougher all around, and the editorial chorus of condemnation gradually neared unanimity. The ranks drew even closer after Botha raised the press-bill sword. Even the *Citizen,* which Perskor had taken over from Alberts in December 1978, vigorously opposed the advocate-general gag.

Faced with this kind of pressure from inside his own party, as well as with an even greater outcry from most other quarters (an International Press Institute representative called the advocate-general "a censor—Dr. Goebbels in a safari suit"),[36] Botha backed down. But only on the Advocate-General Bill. By the time Parliament adjourned in 1979, the other antipress legislation had become law, to wit:

The Police Act Amendment prevents newspapers from publishing any untrue matter about the police.

The Inquests Amendment makes it an offense to prejudice, influence, or anticipate the proceedings or findings of an inquest. Had this been the law when Steve Biko died in detention, the papers would not have been able to report he had died of brain damage.

The National Supplies Procurement Amendment severely

36. " 'Dr. Goebbels in a safari suit,' " *South Africa/Namibia Update,* 13 June 1979, p. 2.

limits reporting on goods and services the government regards as strategic.

The Petroleum Products Amendment similarly limits reporting about oil.

Willem de Klerk, editor of *Die Transvaler*, is among the country's most thoughtful Afrikaner journalists. Not long after Mostert's Muldergate revelations in early November 1978, de Klerk editorialized: "There are always rules. If Afrikaners argue about this then they are betraying their Calvinist faith, their democratic system of government and the civilization they have built here. There may be no interference with the foundation upon which the order has been built."[37] His message collapses around its obvious contradiction, the contradiction at the core of South African life and certainly of the information scandal. The Department of Information aimed to justify the "foundation" of apartheid by, when necessary, breaking the rules. The English-language press had pinned down this contradiction for more than thirty years. With hostile forces besieging South Africa on all sides as the country moved into the 1980s, the Englishers' catechism irritated the Afrikaner more than ever. That, more than anything else, explains why ultimately the English-language press may prove the most serious casualty of Muldergate. Even without the new curbs passed in 1979, the government has more than enough leverage to bring its critics to heel.

37. *Financial Times*, 14 November 1978.

4 The Press Council

The roots of the South African Press Council were planted in 1950, two years after the Nationalists came to power, when the government established a Press Commission of Inquiry. Its mandate called for inspection of a wide range of issues, from tendencies toward monopoly to "the adequacy or otherwise of existing means of self-control and discipline."[1] The commission took almost twelve years to disgorge its first report. A second set of findings appeared in 1964, and together the two reports fill more than seventy-seven hundred typewritten pages. But they provide little more than "documentation" to support the party's antipress line.

The first report dealt primarily with the English-language press's financial superiority over its Afrikaans-language rivals, and the former's links to big business. The second report did not touch on the South African press at all. Instead, it analyzed thousands of clippings and cables filed by full-time foreign correspondents, stringers, and others sending news of the country to the outside world. Cornelius P. Mulder would not organize his image-making machine for ten years, but the commission anticipated the Department of Information's propaganda campaign with mathematical certainty. It found exactly 47.15 percent of the dispatches on political or racial subjects "very bad," 20.10 percent "bad," 25.85 percent "faulty," and only 6.90 percent "good."[2] The commission stated that in the period

1. Alex Hepple, *Press under Apartheid* (London: International Defence and Aid Fund, 1974), p. 9.

2. Elaine Potter, *The Press as Opposition: The Political Role of South African Newspapers* (London: Chatto & Windus, 1975), p. 106.

studied—primarily from May 1950 to July 1955—dispatches failed to recognize the "remarkable extent" of "peace and harmony" between races and language groups in South Africa.[3] Moreover, the commission charged, the reporting covered up the "semi-civilized nature of the Native. The cannibalistic and barbaric acts of violence that are from time to time perpetuated by the Natives are not reported or, if reported, are represented as having resulted from the frustration occasioned by the supposedly unjust, harsh and oppressive treatment meted out to the Natives by the Whites."[4]

The press—both foreign and domestic—did not have to wait until 1962 and 1964 to get a good idea of what was coming. In 1956 another government-appointed body—the Commission of Inquiry in Regard to Undesireable Publications—issued a call for greater control of the press. Among several other devices, it proposed compulsory registration of newspaper, magazine, and book publishers with a government-run publications board. A publication bill, based in part on these recommendations, arrived in Parliament in 1960. It cast the net wide by making it a criminal offense to print, publish, distribute, or sell "any undesireable newspaper." A newspaper fell into the category "if it, or any part of it, prejudicially affects the safety of the State; can have the affect of disturbing the peace or good order; prejudicing the general welfare; being offensive to decency; giving offense to the religious convictions of any section of the inhabitants; bringing any section of the inhabitants into ridicule or contempt; harming relations between sections of the inhabitants . . . *or is otherwise on any ground objectionable*" (italics mine).[5] This sweeping legislation was dropped into the hopper by P. W. Botha, then deputy minister of the interior and by 1978 prime minister.

Both the English and Afrikaans press denounced the bill, and, initially, they got a reprieve. But in 1963 the Nationalists prevailed, and it became law—the Publications and Entertainment Act. Even before passage, the bill achieved one of the government's goals: it sufficiently rattled the country's news-

3. Ibid.
4. Ibid., pp. 106–7.
5. Hepple, *Press under Apartheid,* p. 18.

paper publishers so that in January 1962 their principal organization, the Newspaper Press Union (NPU), drew up a code of conduct and in March established the country's first press council. The code's final clause at the time reflects the publishers' nervousness: "While the press retains its traditional right of criticism, comment should take due cognizance of the complex racial problems of South Africa and should also take into account the general good and the safety of the country and its people."[6]

The NPU was not only worried about the pending Publications and Entertainment Act. It was equally concerned that the government would make good its long-standing threat to establish its own press code and council, one with full legal sanctions. By voluntarily establishing a self-regulatory code and council, the NPU hoped to mollify the Nationalists. And to a degree it did. In return, members of the NPU, which include virtually all the major daily and weekly newspapers in the country, were exempted from the Publications and Entertainment Act when it was passed in 1963. This law, if applied, would have made it altogether impossible for anything approaching a free press to function in South Africa. The act is so broad that even the most patriotic Afrikaner editor would have difficulty not running afoul of it.

Although the government's willingness to exclude the NPU from the catchall Publications Act (so renamed in 1975) appears a liberal move, it is just the opposite. Not only can the Nationalists keep threatening a statutory press code and council, but they can always legislate away the Publications Act exemption as well. The government also knows its other antipress laws conveniently overlap the Publications Act. When the Nationalists determined it was time to act against the *World* and *Weekend World* in 1977, for example, the papers were banned and their editor, Percy Qoboza, detained under terms of the country's Internal Security Act. By exempting the NPU from the Publications Act, the Nationalists also calmed the Afrikaans-language newspapers, which, however politically loyal to the government, resented the press restrictions. The NPU-Nationalist trade-off on the Publications Act also leaves small

6. Ibid., p. 18.

periodicals outside the publishers' organization at the mercy of the government. Since the act's passage in 1963, the Nationalists have systematically expunged all attempts to establish even moderately left journals.

The South African Society of Journalists (SASJ), the country's principal reporters' union, unanimously rejected the code and council in 1962. The society maintained the publishers had jeopardized journalistic independence in collusion with the government. The NPU, which approved the scheme twenty-five managements to seven, argued primarily that whatever the unhappiness over the code and council they were preferable to the threatened statutory restrictions. The *Rand Daily Mail,* which vigorously opposed the council, called this lesser-of-two-evils approach "surrender by installment."[7] More recently, Hans Strydom, news editor of the *Sunday Times* and a former president of SASJ, called it "rape by assent." Strydom, like many of his colleagues, feels that the NPU collapsed in the face of threats. "You're dealing with a dangerous, ruthless bunch of politicians," he says. "They know what they're doing. To let them in the door just makes trouble."[8]

And there was no end to the trouble. At a Nationalist party congress in Cape Town in September 1973, Prime Minister Vorster told the press to put its house in order by January 1974 or face statutory controls. The mere threat of legislative action proved enough. The NPU quickly took refuge in self-censorship by giving its council power to levy fines of up to $11,600.

No bill was introduced when Parliament convened in 1974. But Nationalist displeasure with the press continued, and in March 1977 the government did introduce a press bill that, if enacted, would have supplanted the NPU's code and council. It called for still stricter penalties and set down some new offenses, but these were so vaguely defined that enforcement seemed unworkable. After several weeks of tense negotiations between the NPU and the Nationalists, the government withdrew the bill, promising to introduce it again in a year if the press did not behave. Again, the NPU responded by tightening its code with the promise to exercise "due care and responsibil-

7. *Rand Daily Mail,* 14 March 1962.
8. Interview with Hans Strydom, Johannesburg, 22 October 1978.

ity" when treating such delicate subjects as race relations, "violence and atrocities."[9] By the time Vorster's probationary year passed, the Muldergate revelations were beginning to spill out—not a particularly propitious time to reintroduce antipress legislation, however much the government might have liked to.

The British Press Council and the National News Council in the United States take pains to distance themselves from the newspaper establishment they are designed to keep watch on. The South African Press Council, on the other hand, is practically a subsidiary of the Newspaper Press Union. As spelled out in the organization's constitution, the council consists of a chairman, alternate chairman, and two eight-member panels. The chairman and the alternate must be a judge or retired judge, the executive council of the NPU deciding which. If a judge, the appointment is made by the chief justice of South Africa; if a retired judge, by the NPU executive council itself. The NPU also names both panels: one made up of "persons experienced in the conduct of press affairs . . . in senior administrative or editorial capacities"; the other of "persons capable of representing the interests of the general public."[10] The Press Council shares office space in downtown Johannesburg with the NPU, which also underwrites the council's budget. Gerhard Uys, general manager of the NPU, is registrar of the council. Given these facts, plus the council's history of capitulation to Nationalist legislative threats, it is difficult to reconcile the conclusion by former Judge O. Galgut, the chairman, that the council "is independent of the Government and independent of the Press."[11]

In the council's first six years (1962–68), only 15 complaints were filed, 12 by Nationalist politicians or bureaucrats and Afrikaner organizations.[12] In the decade that followed, however, the number of complaints grew as the council became a fixture on the journalistic landscape. (In 1971, even the South African Society of Journalists formally, if reluctantly, recognized the

9. Kelsey Stuart, *The Newspaperman's Guide to the Law,* 2d ed. (Durban: Butterworth & Co., 1977), p. 267.

10. Ibid., pp. 262–63.

11. O. Galgut, *Report by the Chairman of the South African Press Council* (Johannesburg: South African Press Council, 1978), p. 10.

12. Potter, *Press as Opposition,* p. 111.

council.) According to the annual report of the council for the year ending 29 April 1978, the organization received a total of 253 complaints. However, this numerical leap is deceptive, for as council chairman Galgut himself stresses in the report, "a very large number of complaints have little or no merit." Of the 253 complaints, Judge Galgut summarily dismissed 86 for this reason. Another 91 complaints simply lapsed because those who filed them submitted their evidence late or failed to follow up entirely. "It appears," said Judge Galgut, "that many persons are satisfied once they know that their complaint has been brought to the notice of the newspaper and has been noted by the council. Hence they seek no further action."

Of the remaining 76 complaints 49 were settled between parties, mostly after the offending newspaper ran a correction and/or apology. An additional 17 complaints were still being processed at the end of April 1978. Thus, of the 253 complaints filed in the year-long period, only 10 ultimately were placed before the council for a hearing. In his report on the twelve months, Judge Galgut concluded that in "regard to the millions of words printed daily and the dictates of urgency in getting the newspaper printed, the number of complaints in which the newspapers erred and conceded their errors is insignificant. This also applies to the number of matters which upon adjudication were decided against the newspapers." He also observed that in no case did he feel called upon to punish a newspaper with the $11,600 fine he is empowered to levy, adding that the most severe penalty he imposed all year was a reprimand.

Still, when the government wanted to exploit the council, it proved a handy tool. Out of the ten complaints heard, a majority were filed by Nationalist interests. In early 1978, for example, Eschel Rhoodie was still riding high as secretary of information and was upset by a paragraph in a February 19 article in the *Sunday Express*, which read: "*To The Point* has strong connections with the Department of Information, whose Secretary, Dr. Eschel Rhoodie, became its first editor in 1972 and whose present editor, Mr. John Poorter, was Director of Information at the SA Embassy in London." The *Express* voluntarily responded to the secretary's complaint on February 26 with an article under the headline, "Rhoodie protests to Express":

Dr. Rhoodie says he was assistant editor of *To The Point* (and not the first editor as we reported) for nine months in 1972—six years ago. He does not dispute the statement that the present editor of *To The Point,* Dr. John Poorter, was once one of the Department of Information's top men at the South African Embassy in London. Before Dr. Rhoodie worked as assistant editor of *To The Point,* he was employed by the Department of Information. When he ceased to be assistant editor, he rejoined the department and in 1976 he told the [Durban] *Daily News* that the department spent [$5,800 a year on copies of] the magazine. Dr. Rhoodie also gave figures for purchases of *The Star, Rand Daily Mail* and *The Citizen* which—compared with respective circulation figures—showed that proportionately more was being spent by the department on *To The Point* than on the other papers.

In the light of the above information, the *Sunday Express* believes it was justified in referring to strong connections between the Department of Information and *To The Point.* Dr. Rhoodie protests against this statement. Readers can judge for themselves.

Not satisfied, Rhoodie pressed his complaint with the Press Council. After a hearing on 14 April 1978, Judge Galgut found in his favor. He ruled that the *Express* had not supported its observations about *To the Point* by facts or indicated that they constituted opinion. In addition, Galgut said the *Express* had "failed to inform its readers, as requested in the complaint, that there had been two previous findings by the Press Council [against the Afrikaans-language newspapers *Beeld* and *Rapport* in 1976] which had stated categorically that there was no connection between the Department of Information and *To The Point.*"[13] Judge Galgut ordered the *Express* to publish this adjudication "with due prominence." By late October Eschel Rhoodie was packing to flee the country, and his sidekick, J. van Z. Alberts, publisher of *To the Point,* had been exposed as one of the Department of Information's principal propagandists and front men. By the end of April 1979 the government had conceded that *To the Point* was one of the Department of Infor-

13. Galgut, *Report on Complaint No. 27/2/78,* (Johannesburg: South African Press Council, 1978), p. 5.

mation's secret projects, and put the cost to taxpayers of running the seven-year-old magazine at more than $16 million.[14]

The government goes after its own newspapers through the council as well. *Rapport,* the largest Afrikaans-language paper in the country, reported on 28 May 1978 that East Rand police were investigating a possible connection between the Department of Information scandal and the murder the previous November of Dr. Robert Smit and his wife. Smit was the economist who allegedly told friends that when he became finance minister he planned to expose corruption that went right to the top. *Rapport* was the first paper to even suggest a link between the deaths and Muldergate. The police instituted proceedings before the Press Council, demanding the name of *Rapport*'s informant. The newspaper did not divulge the source but on 19 November 1978 published a page-one apology for its Smit story.

Six months passed between *Rapport*'s Smit story and apology. But when the good image of South Africa hangs in the balance, the government can get same-day service from the council. After Minister of Justice James Kruger read the *Rand Daily Mail* of 7 October 1977, he phoned Judge Galgut and persuaded him to call an urgent hearing. At issue was the *Mail*'s dogged pursuit of the cause of Steve Biko's death in detention on September 12. Kruger took angry exception to the paper's page-one headline ("No sign of hunger strike—Biko doctors") and a paragraph in the article that read: "The facts that emerged from interviews with these doctors and others who had contact with Mr. Biko during the last week of his life contradict points made by Mr. Kruger in the statement that followed the world-wide outcry over Mr. Biko's death." In his follow-up letter of complaint, Kruger said an urgent hearing was of "national importance because . . . the overseas news media are taking over [*sic*] everything that is being written about the Biko case in the South African English Press."[15] Sydney Kentridge, a highly esteemed South African lawyer and counsel for the Biko family, defended the *Mail.* But by the end of the day, the council decided the paper's performance deserved a reprimand, and

14. *Rand Daily Mail,* 1 May 1979.
15. *Johannesburg Star,* 8 October 1977.

Judge Galgut handed one down. It criticized the *Mail* for its performance and ordered the paper to run a correction on page one.

The South African Press Council's leverage ultimately comes not from its procedural powers but from the circumstances of its establishment and the fact of its continuing existence. When the Nationalists need it, it is there—as the experience of the *Express, Rapport,* and *Mail* clearly demonstrates. That is hardly to say the South African press is perfect. Like journalism elsewhere in the world, it is sometimes imprecise, lacking in nuance, or just plain wrong. If South Africa were a truly democratic country, an independent press council might prove a useful corrective—as they do in Britain and the United States. But in the repressive atmosphere fostered by Pretoria, the South African Press Council is little more than a weapon the state uses to intimidate its critics.

5 The Legal Labyrinth

Within instant reach of every South African reporter and editor is a publication entitled *The Newspaperman's Guide to the Law.* This well-organized volume provides a crucial guide for the journalist threading his way through the minefield of press legislation laid down by the government over more than three decades. The bible of the profession, it is probably consulted more than dictionaries and stylebooks combined. Compiled and written by Kelsey W. Stuart, a prominent Johannesburg lawyer, the *Guide* methodically marks the way in a calm and scholarly tone that mutes the author's true feelings about these antipress laws. That he leaves largely to James Madison. In an epigraph Stuart quotes the American president's observation that a "popular government without popular information or means of acquiring it, is but a prologue to a farce or a tragedy or perhaps both."[1]

In South Africa, both. When sports fan Donald Woods, the banned, self-exiled *Daily Dispatch* editor, submitted his all-star cricket team selection to the *Rand Daily Mail,* the editors got nervous and called Stuart. Since it is illegal to quote a banned person, Stuart advised the paper not to publish Woods's team—and it did not. Such high farce, however, is far over-shadowed by the tragic effect of the banning, imprisonment, torture, and general harassment of journalists that take place daily in the name of the law. All major newspapers employ house counsel specifically to handle their queries on what they

1. Kelsey Stuart, *The Newspaperman's Guide to the Law,* 2d ed. (Durban: Butterworth and Co., 1977), p. ix.

47

can and cannot get away with. Stuart, who represents SAAN and has been doing this sort of work for thirty years, estimates he gets an average of five requests for guidance every day. "Friday's a very bad day because of the Sunday papers," he says.[2]

The legal traps set for South African journalists come in various shapes and sizes. They number about two dozen pieces of major legislation, the most deadly of which is the Internal Security Act. Though called the Suppression of Communism Act when first passed in 1950, it effectively covered a good deal more than that right from the start. Besides declaring the Communist party illegal, it gave the state president the power to term unlawful any other organization he thought furthered the aims of communism as defined in the act. But as with so many South African laws, that meant almost anything the government wanted it to mean. For example, the act stretched "communism" all the way to "the encouragement of hostility between the European and non-European races" that could lead to "disturbance or disorder."[3]

More such omnibus provisions were added when the law was converted to the Internal Security Act in 1976; the most odious allows for "preventive detention," or "internment," for twelve-month periods. This provision not only keeps most journalists from getting too inquisitive or outspoken but also frustrates their efforts to cover stories about hundreds of South Africans intimidated or arrested by the government. The act provides for a review committee to investigate, in camera, any internment order, but only government officials may inspect the committee's records. Moreover, none of the powers of the act may be tested in open court. Thus, the judiciary can never be required to define the law's pivotal phrase: "endanger the security of the State and the maintenance of public order."[4]

If a publication dares pierce this vague perimeter, the state president may—under Section 6 of the Internal Security Act—simply shut it down. The government need furnish no reason. It gave none when it closed the left-wing *Guardian* in May 1952

2. Interview with Kelsey Stuart, Johannesburg, 23 October 1978.
3. Stuart, *Newspaperman's Guide*, p. 125.
4. Ibid., p. 130.

after a secret investigation. The weekly quickly reappeared on the stands as the *Clarion*, and with equal speed the government banished it. In October 1952, the paper returned as the *Advance*, and this time lasted two years before the government suppressed it by decree on 22 October 1954. The following week, the periodical's tenacious editor, Brian Bunting, was publishing yet again, this time under the name *New Age*. (The name-change ploy has a long history. In 1897, the revered Afrikaner leader Paul Kruger ordered the Johannesburg *Star* closed for three months after he was lampooned in a cartoon. The newspaper reappeared immediately as the *Comet*—its content unchanged.) *New Age* lasted eight years, until 1962—despite constant harassment and a chronic shortage of funds—when the Suppression of Communism Act was amended to make illegal the reappearance of banned publications under new names. By the end of the year *New Age* was silenced. Despite the new amendment, the paper tried to revive itself once more as *Spark*, but B. J. Vorster, minister of justice at the time, slapped it down again, once and for all.

By the early 1970s any journals that even suggested left-wing sentiments had been virtually wiped away. A key implement was a 1962 amendment to the Suppression of Communism Act that provided that no newspaper could register under the Newspaper and Imprint Act without first depositing up to $23,200 with the government. Unless, that is, the minister of justice "certifies that he has no reason to believe that a prohibition under Section 6 will at any time become necessary in respect to such a newspaper."[5] Thus, any new paper that failed to march to Pretoria's drum was almost surely doomed. By May 1971 the government had demanded deposits from ten applicants. As a result, none could afford to begin publishing.

The Internal Security Act provides for the silencing of individuals with equal efficiency. The minister of justice may arbitrarily "ban" a person whose politics are not regarded as in the best interests of the state. The minister need not give a reason—and usually does not. Banning orders vary in severity, but in essence, they confine the subject to house arrest. Ending

5. Alex Hepple, *Press under Apartheid* (London: International Defence and Aid Fund, 1974), p. 27.

a ban is entirely up to the minister of justice and five years' duration is not uncommon. Amnesty International estimates that the number of persons banned since 1950 is more than thirteen hundred.[6]

Only a small percentage of those banned have been journalists, but the banning system affects the news-gathering process in other ways. The Internal Security Act makes it a crime—punishable by up to three years in prison—to publish "any speech, utterance, writing or statement" by a banned person without the consent of the minister of justice.[7]

The Nationalists announce their bannings and unbannings in the weekly *Government Gazette* (along with such mundane matters as the quality requirements for creamed honey and regulations relating to the artificial insemination of cattle). Journalists ignore this Who's Un-Who at their peril and scour each issue of the *Gazette* to make sure they do not quote a banned person by mistake. "The job of keeping on top of all this is monstrous," said one Johannesburg editor, who then added with a smile that the law did not totally stymie him. His paper and others often get statements once removed, by quoting relatives or friends of the banned person.[8] In general, however, once someone is banned the blackout holds.

The Internal Security Act would seem more than sufficient to cow the more venturesome journalist. But, with overkill typical of the government, the Nationalists have filled South Africa's lawbooks with other legislation designed to stifle free expression. In his *Guide* Stuart lists almost ninety statutes that curb newspaper operations. Some of these, such as libel or copyright laws, are routine; others ar not. The laws described below are among the most actively enforced.

The Terrorism Act of 1967 (as amended). This law makes it a crime to participate in (or encourage) activities ranging from full-scale guerrilla warfare to simply "embarrassing the administration of the affairs of the State."[9] It also makes possession of

6. *Political Imprisonment in South Africa, An Amnesty International Report* (London: Amnesty International Publication, 1978), p. 39.

7. Stuart, *Newspaperman's Guide*, p. 127.

8. Interview with editor who asked not to be identified, Johannesburg, 22 October 1978.

9. Stuart, *Newspaperman's Guide*, pp. 140–41.

ammunition and firearms illegal for would-be "terrorists"—but not for the average white family, whose home almost certainly contains at least a pistol. As Stuart points out, the "impact upon the reporting of news and views . . . is immediately apparent. Letters to the Editor, advertisements, interviews, political columns, leading articles and stories may . . . be construed" as inciting terrorism under the hopelessly broad wording of the law.[10]

The Riotous Assemblies Act of 1956 (as amended). This law makes it illegal to (1) convene or promote prohibited assemblies; (2) record or reproduce speeches by banned persons; (3) encourage feelings of hostility between Europeans and non-Europeans; (4) incite public violence; or (5) foment strikes, boycotts, or other labor unrest. If the minister of justice decrees a violation of the law, the accused faces a prison sentence. For example, if a reporter tape records an antiapartheid speech by a banned person—even if the reporter transgressed inadvertently because he failed to check the *Government Gazette* to determine whether his subject was off limits—he faces up to a year in prison. If it is his second offense, he could get two years.

The Public Safety Act of 1953 (as amended). In 1952 thousands of blacks mounted a "defiance campaign" against apartheid in general and particularly the requirement that they carry passbooks for identification. By the end of the year, some eight thousand had been arrested and the government had formulated this act giving the state president unilateral power to declare a state of emergency and to govern by decree. Under this law, the minister of justice may shut down any news operation he feels contributes to the emergency.

The Criminal Law Amendment Act of 1953 (as amended). This act established harsh penalties for demonstrations against laws in existence. One provision makes it clear that to encourage or incite opposition to specific laws constitutes a violation of the act. Thus, the editor must guard against articles on organizations or individuals advocating—or merely *discussing*— opposition to South Africa's racial laws.

The Official Secrets Act of 1956 (as amended). This act prohibits the communication—in any form—of information on

10. Ibid., p. 141.

matters of national security. The penalty for violation of this act may be as much as fifteen years in prison. Many other nations have similar legislation that puts "official secrets" beyond the reach of reporters. South Africa modeled its act on the British version. The Nationalists, however, use this act to preserve the secrecy of whatever they choose to keep from the public—whether or not such information would affect national security. For example, when Louis Luyt agreed to be the front for the Department of Information's secret financing of the *Citizen*, the deal was sealed under the Official Secrets Act.

The Defense Amendment Act of 1967 (as amended). This law broadens restrictions on the disclosure of military actions. Without permission of the minister of defense, newspapers cannot report on the composition or position of the South African Defense Force (SADF)—the army, navy, air force, and reserves. The press is prohibited from reporting on the SADF in a way "calculated" to embarrass the government in its foreign relations "or to alarm or depress members of the public."[11] The penalty for violation is a prison sentence of up to fifteen years or a maximum fine of $5,800, or both.

The Nationalists feared reporting on their 1975 intervention in Angola's civil war would be detrimental and forbade coverage of the subject under the Defense Amendment Act. While the press worldwide reported the SADF's invasion, it was not publicly known in South Africa. More than any other paper, the *Cape Times* tried to challenge the government. On 17 November 1975 the daily put the following statement on page one: "The Department of Defense last night prohibited publication of a dispatch by the *Cape Times* London correspondent which reported British Sunday newspaper accounts of alleged developments in the Angola civil war. . . . This action, which deprives South African readers of reports available to millions of people abroad, was taken in terms of the Defense Act." On November 29 P. W. Botha, then minister of defense, denied categorically that South African troops were fighting in Angola. So did Prime Minister Vorster in his New Year's message to the people. Yet according to a government report released on 30 April 1976, the biggest battle of the invasion went on for four

11. Ibid., p. 132.

52

days beginning December 9. When the troops finally withdrew from Angola in early 1976, reporters were permitted to witness the prime minister reviewing them. "How," asked one editor, "do you tell your readers about the review without telling them about the war?"[12]

The Prisons Act of 1959 (as amended). The worst excesses of the Nationalist government take place behind prison walls. Torture—though extralegal—is routine. Steve Biko's beating and death on 12 September 1977 were not an isolated case. Between 1963 and 1976 at least twenty-five other prisoners—all blacks—died in political detention. According to government officials, eleven committed suicide, most by hanging themselves in their cells; two fell from high windows during interrogation; one fell down some stairs; one slipped in the shower; one died from thrombosis; four died of causes "unknown" or "undisclosed," and five of "natural causes."[13] Such transparent "explanations" cry out for investigation, as do the accounts of constant physical and emotional abuse in the prison system.

In the 1950s, the English-language papers occasionally attempted such stories. One one occasion, *Drum* managed to penetrate Johannesburg's Central Prison and to come away with a photograph of black prisoners forced to dance around in the nude during a search for contraband. To put such material beyond reach of the press, the government passed the Prisons Act in 1959. The act makes it unlawful to draw a sketch or take a photograph of a prison or prisoners without written permission from the commissioner of prisons. A journalist violates Section 44(f) of this law if he or she "publishes or causes to be published in any manner whatsoever any false information concerning the behavior or experience in prison of any prisoner or ex-prisoner or concerning the administration of any prison, knowing the same to be false, or without taking reasonable steps to verify such information (the onus of proving that reasonable steps were taken . . . being upon the accused)."[14]

This law proved sufficient to chill prison muckraking for

12. Interview with editor who asked not to be identified, Cape Town, 31 October 1978.

13. "South Africa—A 'Police State?' " (Braamfontein: Christian Institute of South Africa, 1976), p. 11.

14. Stuart, *Newspaperman's Guide*, p. 59.

more than five years. Then, in 1965, the *Rand Daily Mail* published a three-part series (June 30–July 2) based on the revelations of Harold Strachan, a recently released white political prisoner. Written by Benjamin Pogrund, then a senior reporter on the *Mail*, the articles portrayed a grim system that condoned everything from unhygienic and overcrowded cells to solitary confinement and systematic brutality. Laurence Gander, then the paper's editor, called on the authorities to begin an immediate investigation of the prison system and promised to publish further revelations if they did not.

The government responded instantly—by raiding the *Mail*. On July 2 police barged into the paper's offices, seizing manuscripts and notes dealing with prison conditions in an unsuccessful attempt to prevent publication of the final article in the series. The government refused to investigate the prisons, and Gander kept his word. On July 30 the *Mail* published sworn statements by several men with prison experience, including J. A. Theron, head warder at the Cinderella Prison at Boksburg. He stated: "I have seen shock treatment being given to convicts at Cinderella Prison to make them give statements. . . . Convicts are told to undress completely. Then they are put on a table covered with a waterproof . . . previously . . . made wet. Water is thrown on the convict. Other prisoners hold the convict down—by his hands and his legs. Then the treatment starts. The warders do it anywhere. They put one button on the convict's body and move the other button away from the body and bring it back in another place—sometimes on his private parts. When the convict starts screaming they put it on his lips to keep his mouth closed. The convict usually screams like hell."

For his candor Theron was suspended from duty in early August and told not to communicate with either prisoners or prison officials. Fourteen months later he was discharged from the Prisons Department. Strachan was convicted for making false statements about prison conditions and sentenced to two and a half years in jail in January 1966. To silence him immediately following the *Mail* disclosures, the government banned him for five years in July 1965. The ban was renewed for another five years in July 1970.

54

Punishing the "squealers" was clearly the Nationalists top priority. But they had no intention of letting Gander and Pogrund off the hook. In August 1965 their passports were revoked. Two years after the series appeared, on 23 June 1967, they were formally charged under Section 44(f) of the Prisons Act. Two years after that, on 10 July 1969, they were found guilty on two counts: publishing false information and failing to take reasonable steps to verify their reporting.

According to Gander, the *Mail* went to "considerable lengths to check and crosscheck the material" and in several instances supported its allegations about prison conditions with sworn affidavits.[15] The presiding judge conceded that some of the *Mail*'s charges were true and that neither Gander nor Pogrund had published the alleged falsities knowingly. Pogrund received a three-month suspended sentence on each count and Gander a $116 fine (or three months) on each count. But the real punishment was in their ordeal and the legal cost to SAAN of nearly $300,000.

In his decision against the *Rand Daily Mail*, the judge left totally unclear what constitutes the "reasonable steps" a paper must take to legally verify its reporting under the strictures of the Prisons Act. Consequently, according to Stuart, "for more than ten years no newspaper has published a report about prisons, their administration or the experience in them of prisoners or ex-prisoners except such reports as place the Prisons Department in a favorable light."[16]

The Publications Act of 1963 (as amended). As explained earlier, this act prohibits publication and distribution of "any undesirable newspaper." All major daily and weekly newspapers are exempt from this legislation by virtue of their membership in the NPU. The act carries a great deal of power nonetheless, for all publications not members of the NPU are naked to its elastic definition of "undesirable." In 1976, for example, the government used the act to close twenty-eight periodicals published by university students around the country. In nine of these cases, possessing the publications was also prohibited. The following year, forty-two student publications,

15. Hepple, *Press under Apartheid*, p. 40.
16. Stuart, *Newspaperman's Guide*, p. 66.

posters, and pamphlets fell to the Publications Act. At the University of Stellenbosch, the student newspaper, *Die Matie*, drew the only possible conclusion, editorializing that it was hard to regard the bannings "as anything other than a determination to close all channels left to students to voice critical or penetrating opinions."[17]

That South African reporters function at all in the maze of restrictive laws the Nationalists have produced is remarkable. That many continue to speak out against the government at mounting risk is astonishing. That dozens of journalists have paid, are paying, and will pay a heavy price for their courage is certain. For not everyone gets such light sentences as Pogrund and Gander—especially if they are black.

17. *Die Matie*, 15 August 1977.

6 "Nothing Remains but Anger"

Nonwhite journalists played a critical role in getting news out of Soweto during the uprising there in June 1976. Unlike their white colleagues, they had access to the township and were able to give vent in print and pictures to the anger and frustration of the population. And they did so again during and after the renewed antigovernment protests that marked the riots' anniversary in 1977. But by that time Minister of Justice of Police and of Prisons J. M. Kruger had finally had enough. On 19 October 1977, as part of his wide-ranging clampdown on the black consciousness movement, he closed the *World* and *Weekend World.* He detained Percy Qoboza, editor of the two papers; Aggrey Klaaste, news editor of the *World;* and Thenjiwe Mtintso, a reporter with the *East London Daily Dispatch* (whose white editor, Donald Woods, was banned that day for five years). That brought to twelve the number of nonwhite journalists detained in 1977, and by year's end at least two more were sent to prison by Kruger's decreee. Among the ten black consciousness organizations banned by Kruger on October 19 was the Union of Black Journalists (UBJ). When twenty-nine newsmen and women marched in Johannesburg on November 30 to protest the bannings and detentions, they were all arrested under the Riotous Assemblies Act, and each was fined $58. Of these actions, Kruger commented that "People who believe the government will allow itself to be intimidated or prescribed to are making a big mistake."[1]

1. "On the Brink of Violence, So Kruger Acted," *South African Digest,* 28 October 1977, p. 2.

Joseph Thloloe joined the reporting staff of the *World* on 1 February 1977. One month later police came to his home in Soweto and arrested him under Section 6 of the Terrorism Act. Thloloe had been active in the UBJ since its founding in 1973, when he was a reporter on *Drum*. At the time of his arrest, he was the UBJ's president. The police made it clear that they wanted to know what he could tell them about the so-called Bethal 18, a group of black activists on trial for allegedly aiding the banned Pan-Africanist Congress. Some of the defendants were Thloloe's friends, and he had met several others. When the executive committee of the UBJ sought to discuss Thloloe's incarceration with the minister of police, he refused on the ground that the detention was unrelated to Thloloe's journalistic duties. The government never stated why he was detained— neither before, during, nor after Thloloe's eighteen-month imprisonment. His jailers kept him in solitary confinement the entire time. His wife and two children were permitted to visit only once, after about fifteen months. He was released on 1 September 1978, and five weeks later he still looked haggard and very weak. When asked how he had been treated, he replied apologetically, "That's not for publication. I can't prove any of the allegations I make simply because I was by myself with the police almost all the time."[2]

Peter Magubane, a black photographer for the *Rand Daily Mail*, was less reluctant to describe his treatment behind bars. In more than twenty years of harassment, Magubane has suffered a broken nose, a five-year banning, and a total of 709 days in detention. He was jailed for 123 days not long after his coverage of the Soweto uprising in June 1976. "I wasn't abused, except when I was interrogated," he recalled:

> They made me stand on three bricks measuring about a foot from the ground. Now you can't stand still because the bricks wobble. I stood on these bricks for five days and five nights without a wink of sleep. They gave me black coffee right through the night and kept changing interrogation teams every two hours. Finally, I began passing blood. Only then did they decide to call the chief interrogating officer, who gave me tablets to ease my pain. That was the

2. Interview with Joseph Thloloe, Johannesburg, 25 October 1978.

end of it, but they kept reminding me: "Your paper, the *Rand Daily Mail,* says we shock people. Do you see any electric shock equipment here? Why don't we beat you up? We let you stand on bricks. Now when you come out of here you tell them that we don't beat and shock people." But other prisoners were definitely shocked and beaten. I think I got better treatment because I was a journalist.[3]

When Magubane returned to Soweto in June 1977, the police picked him up again. They wanted to know how he knew there would be a demonstration marking the anniversary of the protests. After an hour of questioning, Magubane was released—but not before his film was confiscated. The *Rand Daily Mail* protested the incident to the minister of justice, to no avail. Nor was the paper able to persuade the minister to renew Magubane's press card, which had expired shortly after he was released from detention on 28 December 1976. Magubane said that his employers have not protested vigorously enough, but he has become wryly philosophical about the matter. He pointed out, with a smile, that in the days before his press card expired, a policeman would simply hold the document in one hand and, with the other, clobber his face with a gun butt.

While Magubane was still in jail, toward the end of 1976, his journalistic colleagues asked prison authorities to allow him to choose some photographs for submission to the annual Stellenbosch Farmers' Winery Award, among the most prestigious honors for reporters in South Africa. The request was denied. Should he win, they were told, he would not be able to pick up his prize. But Magubane's friends chose a series of pictures for him, and he did win. He won more praise in 1978 with publication of *Magubane's South Africa,* a book of his photographs depicting the sorrows and joys of his countrymen.[4]

Juby Mayet is a widow and the mother of eight children. She is also one of South Africa's more aggressive colored journalists. In 1976 security police raided her home, confiscating notes and publications. The officer in charge told her to pack a suitcase. She lined up her children in front of the officer, intro-

3. Interview with Peter Magubane, Johannesburg, 24 October 1978.
4. Peter Magubane, *Magubane's South Africa* (New York: Alfred A. Knopf, 1978).

duced them, and told him, "These are the children you are now proposing to deprive of their mother."[5] The officer relented, but on 29 May 1978 Mayet was detained under Section 10 of the Internal Security Act. She was released on October 27, but in December she was banned along with many other antigovernment activists.

When detained, Mayet was chief subeditor of the *Voice*, a bimonthly journal edited by nonwhites that began publication in May 1977. Initially sponsored by the staunchly antiapartheid South African Council of Churches, it ran into difficulty with the government from the start. Several early issues were banned, and on 16 June 1978 the *Gazette* declared certain back issues and all subsequent issues undesirable under the Publications Act. To the government the *Voice* was a militant, antiwhite, radical-left propaganda organ bent on undermining the state and feeding frustrations "to the point of explosion."[6] One specific reason the *Gazette* gave for the banning was the *Voice*'s accusation that "the government was guilty of institutionalised violence."[7] Besides Mayet, several others on the *Voice* staff had been detained. In May 1978 the government detained Zakes Mofokeng, assistant manager of the paper, and Phil Mtimkulu, one of its reporters and a former secretary of the UBJ. A month before, Harry Makubire, a former manager of the *Voice* and executive member of the council of churches, was also detained.

Earlier, in 1977, Mayet and Mtimkulu were charged with theft, for removing the property of an unlawful organization. Following a tip that the UBJ would be banned, they withdrew $2,861 from the organization's bank account on the morning of 19 October 1977. Under the Internal Security Act, all assets of a banned organization flow immediately to the government—a provision that has prompted more than one observer to question where the theft charge properly lies. Mayet and Mtimkulu were acquitted because they had withdrawn the money by 9:30 A.M. The magistrate ruled that since the *Gazette* banning the UBJ

5. London *Observer*, 25 June 1978.
6. *Survey of Race Relations in South Africa, 1978* (Johannesburg: South African Institute of Race Relations, 1979), p. 135.
7. Ibid.

was not available to the public until 10:05 A.M. the money had not been withdrawn from an unlawful organization.

Two weeks after its banning, the *Voice* received a stay pending an appeal. But the reprieve came only on the condition that the paper deliver a copy of each issue to the directorate of publications, arbiter of the Publications Act, within hours of its printing. After the *Voice* complied for eleven editions, the government lifted its ban without waiting for the appeal.

At the time of the banning, Revelation Ntouli, editor of the *Voice*, said that the "government will not tolerate any authentic black voices other than those created by the apartheid laws."[8] He also accused the NPU of stalling on the *Voice*'s May 1977 membership application. Had the *Voice* been a member of the NPU, it would have been exempt from the Publications Act. The general manager of the NPU denied the allegation. But only after the ban was lifted in August 1978 did the NPU finally admit the *Voice*.

The banning and unbanning of the *Voice* typifies the carrot-and-stick approach the Nationalists often employ to keep the press in line. After shutting down the *World* and *Weekend World* on October 19, the government did nothing to prevent the Argus Company from publishing its papers a week later under a new logo, the *Post*. But more changed than the name. Before Kruger called Percy Qoboza a "fat, overgrown lout"[9] and closed his papers, the *World* had adopted a uniquely hard line for a mass circulation daily that reached deep into the nonwhite community. In the months following the 1976 Soweto uprising, Qoboza and the *World* spoke with increasing force and clarity about the nation's racial collision course. In addition, *World* reporters brought hard news out of Soweto and the other black townships—news that embarrassed the government, news that few, if any, white journalists could get. When the papers resurfaced as the *Post*, they looked much the same as before—but the zealous political commitment had evaporated almost entirely.

Qoboza sadly concedes the change: "Our press is much less vigorous than it used to be. I have to face the fact that I've had two newspapers shut down and I, myself, have been in jail.

8. *East London Daily Dispatch*, 16 June 1978.
9. "Press Under Attack," *Focus*, 14 January 1978, p. 10.

And some of my colleagues are still in jail. I have to deal with the fact that I still don't know *why* my newspapers were closed down. And why I was taken to jail. And now I'm editing a newspaper very much blindfolded. The minister of justice continues merely to tell us that we know what we have done, and that's all. When we ask him for specifics there is no response at all."[10] Qoboza's detention lasted just under five months. Relatively speaking, he was treated well. His wife could visit him twice a week and books and newspapers were available. That is because his arrest came under Section 10 of the Internal Security Act. "It's the people under Section 6 of the Terrorism Act that I worry about," Qoboza says. "You are literally banished from the face of the earth. Your family has no access to you. Your lawyers have no access to you. Your doctors have no access to you. Like Joe Thloloe."[11]

White journalists are harassed less frequently and punished less harshly than nonwhites. For example, Kruger closed down the *World* and jailed Percy Qoboza; he allowed the *East London Daily Dispatch* to continue publishing and banned Donald Woods. Occasionally, however, the Nationalists apply their notion of justice with a fierce evenhandedness. Anthony Holiday is a white South African. In 1976, he was a reporter on the *Cape Times*. Unknown to his editor, Anthony Heard, Holiday was also an activist with the African National Congress. "He was mailing out incendiary stuff that in any free society would amount to routine dissent," said Heard. "But here it was bound to cause trouble." Heard added that he would have fired Holiday had he known of his political activities.[12] Holiday was detained under Section 6 of the Terrorism Act on 28 July 1976, convicted less than four months later, and locked up in Pretoria Central Prison for a term of six years.

Short of detention or banning, South African journalists—white and nonwhite—face a wide range of petty and not-so-petty harassments. Police frequently hector "unfriendly" reporters covering sensitive stories—such as political trials—by barring access to the courtroom. Sometimes the police act arbi-

---

10. Interview with Percy Qoboza, Johannesburg, 24 October 1978.
11. Ibid.
12. Interview with Anthony Heard, Cape Town, 31 October 1978.

trarily at the scene, sometimes they refuse to grant or renew press credentials. For example, in 1978, a reporter from a major daily had been abused by police and kept from covering a trial of Soweto students because he did not have a press pass. A top editor at the paper called a high security police official to ask whether a letter from the editor would be sufficient. A letter would do, the official allowed, and the polite exchange ended. After hanging up the phone, the editor said, "Part of the madness of this country is that he's been telling everyone for years that he's determined to get me behind bars."[13]

Another part of the madness is the tapping of telephones. "Sitting in the [Durban Sunday] Tribune's Pretoria office one day, I received a call from the news editor, Eugene Hugo," recalled Martin Schneider, now political editor of the Rand Daily Mail. "We discussed progress on a number of stories and covered delicate and intimate details connected with them. Our conversation over, we replaced our receivers. Hugo then dialed out another call, but, as he started, he heard part of our earlier conversation repeated. Obviously, it had been taped."[14] Journalists on English-language papers now accept tapped telephones as a routine hazard of their profession.

Routine, too, is the banning of books and periodicals. According to the United Nation's Unit on Apartheid, more than twenty thousand titles apparently threaten the fabric of the Republic of South Africa. Given the country's frantic fear of communism, many on the list are understandable: Quotations from Chairman Mao Tse-tung, Soviet Marxism by Herbert Marcuse, and Class Struggle in Africa by Kwame Nkrumah. On the list as well are hundreds of titles that offend the Afrikaner's Calvinist sense of propriety. Few discoveries appear to delight immigration officials more than an issue of Playboy or Penthouse in a traveler's luggage. Even without pictures, sex will not do. Books considered too lascivious range from manuals like How to Get More Out of Sex by Dr. David Reuben and Cosmopolitan's Love Book by Helen Gurley Brown to Miss Lonelyhearts by Nathanael West and A Month of Sundays by John Updike. Possession of

13. Exchange at which author was present, Johannesburg, 24 October 1978.
14. Martin Schneider, "Truth Victim of Press Laws," More, December 1977, p. 15.

banned literature is punishable by fine or imprisonment.

The government keeps a particularly close watch on journalists since they act as conduits for the ideas and information carried in the banned material. To keep track of the government's banning decisions, all major newspapers subscribe to *Jacobsens: "Always Up To Date Index of Objectionable Literature."* The editors of *Jacobsens* monitor the weekly announcements in the *Government Gazette,* arrange all changes in alphabetical order, and then send out new pages to their subscribers, who substitute them for the outdated ones in *Jacobsen*'s convenient looseleaf binders.

On 18 January 1978 Amnesty International published a 108-page report entitled *Political Imprisonment in South Africa.* On January 26 the government banned it as an "undesirable publication." Most South Africans will never see this damning indictment of the Nationalist party's enforcement of apartheid. With lucid prose and a handful of sickening photographs depicting beaten and murdered blacks, the report makes a fearful case against the Afrikaner government. In a brief profile of Tenjiwe Ethel Mtintso, the *East London Daily Dispatch* reporter detained on 19 October 1977, the report states:

> In March 1977 Tenjiwe Mtintso appeared at an inquest into the death in detention of Mapetla Mohapi (a prominent member of the Black Consciousness Movement) and gave evidence concerning her own experience in security police custody. [She had been detained in 1976 also.] She said that after her arrest at Kingwilliamstown she was punched in the face and kicked by members of the security police. Later she was interrogated by Captain Hansen, head of the security police in Kingwilliamstown. She was again slapped and punched, and was made to stand for three days and nights during which she was allowed no food, drink or toilet facilities. In September, she was taken to Kei Road police station in Kingwilliamstown, where Mapetla Mohapi had been in custody at the time of his death. It was there, she alleged, that Captain Hansen and another security police officer had placed a wet towel around her face causing partial suffocation. This happened three times. Tenjiwe Mtintso alleges that she was told by Captain Hansen "now you see how Mapetla died." Tenjiwe Mtintso

also alleged that while she was in detention the security police had told her, falsely, that her own child had died.[15]

Mtintso was detained without charge. But any Afrikaner official will say privately that her offense was a political commitment to Steve Biko and the Black Consciousness Movement. She would not deny that. Nor would many other black journalists whose political awareness has been sharpened in the aftermath of the 1976 Soweto upheaval and Biko's death in detention fourteen months later. In South Africa's increasingly polarized racial atmosphere, the line separating objective reporting and political activism grows hazier every day.

"One of the fundamental tenets of the Black Consciousness Movement is that blacks should solidify their own position before dealing with whites,"[16] said journalist Zwelakhe Sisulu, whose father was sentenced in 1964 to life on Robben Island for political crimes. Like most black journalists, Sisulu is a member of the Writers Association of South Africa (WASA), which replaced the UBJ when it was banned on 19 October 1977. For years, the South African Society of Journalists (SASJ) refused to accept black members, opting for union status so it could negotiate for wages with the NPU. (Had the SASJ admitted blacks, it would have become a reporters' association since South African law prohibited mixed race union membership.) The SASJ abandoned its union role a few years ago and agreed to take in nonwhites. But by then, the lines had been drawn and most blacks refused to join, preferring UBJ (now WASA). A measure of the depth of the split between black and white journalists came in July 1978, when the WASA congress at Durban attacked Donald Woods for "the shameless manner in which he is exploiting the name of the hero of the people, Steve Biko." WASA called the banned white editor "irrelevant to the black struggle and to black journalism."[17]

The roster of nonwhite journalists who have been banned, detained, and sometimes tortured in recent years has grown

15. *Political Imprisonment in South Africa, An Amnesty International Report* (London: Amnesty International Publications, 1978), p. 55.
16. Interview with Zwelakhe Sisulu, Johannesburg, 25 October 1978.
17. *Rand Daily Mail*, 3 July 1978.

steadily. From 1976 through 1978 more than two dozen non-white journalists were detained, several more than once. Among them Don Mattera, detained on 23 September 1976. At the time, he was already under a five-year banning order dating back to October 1973. Perhaps because he is colored and not black, he was allowed to continue working as an editor at the *Star,* although he could no longer publish his writing in South Africa. In February 1978, Mattera was arrested and accused of addressing or attending five meetings, in violation of his banning order. In April 1978, a court acquitted him on all five counts. Mattera is a poet as well as a journalist. Not long after his acquittal, the London-based *Index on Censorship* published one of his poems. It reads, in part:

> What dreams and visions we clutched
> in our frantic search for life
> are singed by the heat of our chains
> Nothing remains
> but anger, at ourselves
> at God. . . .

> Reconciliation and amity
> drown in a whirlpool
> of unrelenting dogma.
> What hope existed for a bloodless revolt
> now lies shattered
> into a million fragments
> of despair. . . .

> And if we must weep
> let us weep gently
> committing our pain
> to our cause
> And with one blow
> silence the men
> who laugh as we die[18]

At the end of October 1978, Mattera's banning order expired. Kruger renewed it for five years.

18. Don Mattera, "Scenes from a Banned Life," *Index on Censorship,* September–October 1978, p. 8.

7 Broadcasting, the State Cyclops

On 2 November 1978 Judge Anton Mostert defied Prime Minister Botha and released the evidence that first turned Muldergate from speculation to fact. Dozens of journalists converged on his news conference in Pretoria—not only reporters from the newspapers, which would bulge with the scandal the next day, but also correspondents from the South African Broadcasting Corporation (SABC). Because they could get on the air immediately, these SABC reporters had a scoop on their hands. But both radio and television demurred. Instead, announcers advised listeners and viewers that "the SABC has decided not to broadcast [Mostert's] statement at this stage."[1] By way of explanation they said that under the mandate of the Mostert inquiry, the evidence could be made public only by State President Vorster or if introduced in Parliament.

For months, the SABC had either ignored the Muldergate rumblings or dismissed them as the sour-grapes politicking of the opposition press. The day of Mostert's revelations, J. E. van Zyl, the SABC's director of news services, said that "SABC is biding its time, as requested by the government, until the government reports on the information affair. At this time there are no facts, only newspaper speculation by the SAAN group. The real facts are that the English-language newspapers are in a battle with the government." Besides, van Zyl went on, "this type of story is not visual. The papers say that they have information. We have to *show* that information."[2] By the next after-

1. *Rand Daily Mail,* 3 November 1978.
2. Interview with J. E. van Zyl, Johannesburg, 2 November 1978.

noon Mostert had provided enough information for a fairly compelling rogues' gallery on the nightly news. But the SABC would have none of it.

In general, SABC offers one part news to three parts propaganda—broadcast daily by one of the most state-restricted television industries in the world. The Nationalists make few apologies for television as the cyclops of the state. The 1971 government report that established the ground rules for introduction of television into South Africa maintained that the nation "must have its own television service in order to nurture and strengthen its own spiritual roots, to foster respect and love for its own spiritual heritage, *and to protect and project the South African way of life as it has developed here in its historical context*" (italics mine).[3]

Much of the Afrikaner leadership long saw television as at best an unnecessary social frill and at worst an anti-Calvinist destroyer of the soul. In addition, many Nationalists regarded television as a political threat, a Trojan horse that might kick up all sorts of mischief once let loose in an apartheid Troy. In the mid-1960s Dr. Albert Hertzog, minister of posts and telegraphs, railed against the cult of "the little black box" with typical Afrikaner passion. He depicted Harry Oppenheimer, chairman of the giant mining conglomerate, Anglo-American Corporation, and his protelevision friends, as determined to use "this deadly weapon" to eventually destroy white South Africa by undermining "the morale of the white man."[4]

By the end of the 1960s, however, technological developments had made South African television a political imperative. As the 1971 commission report stated: "the technical possibility that television programmes broadcast via satellites could be picked up direct by the public in South Africa has made it essential for urgent attention to be given by the Government to the possible introduction of a television service in South Africa. If, for instance, it were possible for a hostile power to transmit television programmes to South Africa via

3. *Report of the Commission of Inquiry into Matters Relating to Television* (Pretoria: Government Printer, 1971), p. 48.

4. *New York Times*, 10 November 1964.

satellites, South Africa could only counter this effectively by introducing its own service."[5] After years of a debate that was by no means over, South African television finally flickered to life on 5 January 1976. The evening's fare included "The Bob Newhart Show," a program for children, the Paris Symphony Orchestra, and, just before the religious sign-off, a recorded message from Prime Minister Vorster allowing that he was not overenthusiastic about television.

Vorster's misgivings doubtlessly waned somewhat the following year after his triumph at the polls. In what is known in some circles as the "Great Television Election," the prime minister was returned to office with the biggest majority the Nationalists had ever achieved. His popularity as a tough leader undeniably was a major factor, but SABC left little to chance. As one opposition M.P. observed about the weeks leading up to the 30 November 1977 election, "There has never been a time in the history of South Africa when so many bridges, hospitals, schools, odd institutions here and there and dams were opened by various dignitaries."[6] A Rhodes University survey bears out this preelection blitz. It examined twelve newscasts in English from September 19 to October 10 and found that Nationalist party representatives or government officials received 81 percent of air time given to South African politics. In those same twelve newscasts, non-Nationalist M.P.'s or party members were seen or heard on the screen for only three minutes and twenty seconds, or 4.4 percent of the time. "That is far too much," declared one loyal Nationalist M.P. during a parliamentary wrangle over SABC bias.[7] Later in the same debate, Vorster confidently maintained that had the opposition members been given more coverage "they would have lost even further."[8]

The Progressive Federal party, the chief political opposition, repeatedly has proposed that television be bound by the rules of the South African Press Council, which would at least

5. *Report,* p. 1.
6. *Hansard,* 17 February 1978, col. 1328
7. Ibid., col. 1289.
8. Ibid., col. 1340.

require the Nationalists to be consistent in monitoring print and electronic journalism. But the government is satisfied with the SABC's in-house code, which states, in part:

> Ministerial statements on state policy and ministerial explanations on legislative measures shall be regarded as factual news and dealt with as such. . . .
>
> Comment in the form of statements or explanations may only be broadcast when it originates from a person of authority or an acknowledged expert in a given field. . . .
>
> A political report shall be regarded as *prima facie* contentious and shall be broadcast only if, firstly, it is of a factual and/or authoritative nature; secondly, if it is a positive statement of policy by a political party in respect of any matter of dispute, provided the statement and/or broadcast does not draw comparison with comment on a declared policy of steps followed by any other South African political party.[9]

The African Broadcasting Company, set up in 1927 as a profit-seeking monopoly, was aimed primarily at the English-speaking audience in the major cities. When the Parliament set up the SABC in 1936, the government officially terminated the African Broadcasting Company. But the English-oriented character of South African radio changed little because the English-dominated United party ruled the country. As Peter B. Orlik has observed in his study of the Afrikaner takeover of the SABC:

> [W]hen a member of the Afrikaners' then-minority Nationalist Party rose to complain about the "political speeches of British statesmen" which the [SABC] was airing and to ask whether similar attention was being given to the remarks of South African statesmen, [the United party's] Minister of Posts and Telegraph's [replied] that the remarks by British leaders were broadcast due to their intrinsic international importance. Pronouncements by domestic politicians were, said the Minister, largely vehicles of local and partisan interest and broadcasting of these

9. Ibid., 17 May 1977, cols. 7850–51.

would inject an unwanted element of Party propaganda into the transmissions.[10]

This typically British patronizing posture infuriated many Afrikaners during World War II. For example, Prime Minister Jan Smuts's pro-British United party used the SABC to push the Allied cause, employing radio campaigns to sign up soldiers for a South African army that had lost many men at the battle of Tobruk in 1942. The Nationalists, most of whom were either neutral or—like future Prime Ministers Verwoerd and Vorster—frankly pro-Nazi, had managed to block conscription in Parliament and were enraged by the radio recruiting. Ironically, however, it ultimately proved to their advantage. For many of those who answered Smuts's call to arms were English-speaking staff members of the SABC. By the war's end, Afrikaners filled many of the vacated SABC jobs. Thus, the Nationalist bureaucratization of the SABC began, and when the party took over the government in 1948, the control panels of South African radio came with it.

The SABC offers the most ambitious radio service on the African continent. Broadcasting in both Afrikaans and English, it sends out hundreds of hours of public and cultural affairs shows each week. News programs range from routine weather reports and sports scores to straight forward bulletins and political commentary that advance the Nationalist cause at every opportunity. Music, drama, and religion make up the backbone of cultural programming. In addition to this domestic programming, the SABC beams its External Services via shortwave beyond the country's borders in English, Afrikaans, and more than half a dozen European and African languages. The SABC also operates Radio Bantu, which provides services to the homelands. These FM transmissions go out in many African languages, as do additional services for blacks in South West Africa (Namibia). Throughout its programming, the basic SABC propaganda mission is rarely out of earshot. In its 1977

10. Peter B. Orlik, "South African Broadcasting Corporation: An Instrument of Afrikaner Political Power," *Journal of South African Affairs*, January 1978, pp. 55–64.

71

annual report, the SABC made the following statement about its External Service: "In view of the biased anti-South African campaign being conducted by a large section of the Dutch news media, broadcasts from here called for a more informative approach. . . . The daily magazine programme *Panorama RAS* [was] turned into a highly topical program to counter 'slanted' news against South Africa."[11]

With the arrival of television, the SABC's propaganda impact and potential took a quantum leap. By the end of 1978 well over one million sets saturated white South Africa—almost double the number in Egypt, which by the end of 1976 had already relinquished its position to South Africa as the nation with the most television receivers on the Continent. Peak-hour viewers in 1978 averaged more than two million, which meant that roughly half the country's white population was glued to the single television channel offered by SABC. Few nonwhites can afford television sets, and most of those who can live in townships, like Soweto, that have little or no electricity.

SABC television (and radio) beams across the land from Auckland Park, on the outskirts of Johannesburg, using the most sophisticated and advanced broadcasting equipment in the world. Television broadcasts emanate daily from 6:00 P.M. to 11:30 P.M. (11:00 P.M. on Sundays). Half the programming is in English, half in Afrikaans—with one language coming first one evening, the other language first the next. In a typical week (30 October–5 November 1978), SATV, as the service is called, offered its usual diet of foreign syndication: "Nancy Drew" on Monday, "McCloud" on Tuesday, "Sha Na Na" on Wednesday, "Captains and the Kings" on Thursday, and "Blitspatrollie" on Friday. Over the weekend came "The Return of the Saint," "The Hunchback of Notre Dame," and "The Dream and the Destiny," a documentary about Georges Bizet. Locally produced programs ranged from soap operas and sports programs to game shows and pop music broadcasts, from an exploration of hotel management to the twice nightly news broadcasts served up as objective journalism. Each evening ends with a sermon and reverent nod to the Lord. On one such epilogue,

11. *The 1977 Annual Report of the South African Broadcasting Corporation* (Johannesburg: South African Broadcasting Corporation, 1978), pp. 93–95.

just before the Mostert disclosures, a well-scrubbed young Afrikaner minister cautioned viewers about Christ's love of truth, then pointedly divined the newspapers' failure to practice it.

SATV officials say that they are eager to import better programs and would especially welcome material from the British Broadcasting Corporation (BBC). And the BBC is willing to sell. But British television unions made it clear early on that they would boycott the apartheid state—and they have. For example, the May football cup final is among the biggest sporting events in England. When BBC management raised the possibility of selling the broadcast of the game to South Africa via satellite, the unions vowed to black out the broadcast in Great Britain. BBC officials bowed to the threat. The Nationalists point to this as yet another example of the hypocritical discrimination South Africa faces, noting that the unions are perfectly willing to deal with the Soviet Union.

Should the British unions ever relent, South African viewers can count on getting a good deal more of "Masterpiece Theatre" than of public affairs programming. SATV's loyal Afrikaner program directors certainly would not schedule such fare as "The White Tribes of Africa," the BBC's four-part documentary on Southern Africa. Just the filming of it in 1978 made Pretoria so nervous that at one point the government threatened to withdraw the crew's work permits unless the BBC agreed to show a South African-produced film with the "White Tribes" series when it ran in England. The BBC countered by pulling its crew out of South Africa, and the government ultimately allowed them to return and finish the series.

So starved are some South Africans for this kind of independent programming that they have purchased expensive video tape recorders and, at considerable additional cost, fly in cassettes to play on them. These range from blue movies to political documentaries, and the importer risks fine or imprisonment for his actions (as does anyone who comes to his home to view this contraband). In 1977, when the U.S. International Communications Agency (ICA) showed the television version of Alex Haley's black family history, "Roots," its auditoriums were mobbed. "All the audiences were mixed race and the reaction was incredible," recalls Steven McDonald, political officer at the U.S. embassy in Pretoria.[12] Prime Minister Vorster telephoned U.S. Ambassador William B. Edmondson to protest, calling the Haley saga inflammatory. But the series ran to completion. The ICA considered running the series again in 1978, but—after talks with Washington—Ambassador Edmondson said no.

Blacks are a rarity on SATV. For many months in the late 1970s, the most popular local program was "The Villagers," a serial about a gold-mining town. No black actors or actresses appeared in the programs, although gold has always been mined almost entirely by blacks. After considerable debate, SATV ran the National Theatre of Great Britain's film version of *Othello* (22 October 1978), which shows love across the color line. Shakespeare, plus the fact that the "black" Moor was only Laurance Olivier temporarily darkened for the occasion, helped get this one by the censors.

Almost without exception, nonwhites who appear on public affairs programs either support the government or are at most politely critical of it. Occasionally, though, an outspoken critic will slip through the bureaucratic net. On 20 September 1978, on the interview program "Midweek," Bishop Desmond Tutu, general secretary of the antiapartheid South African Council of Churches, openly attacked the government. Tutu was "amazed" the taped interview had gone on the air; so was the SATV hierarchy, which sharply reprimanded the men responsible for the indiscretion.[13]

The censors were more typically alert when reviewing a thirty-five minute documentary on Crossroads, the 140-acre squatter settlement in Cape Town. The film is a sympathetic portrait of a black community threatened by a government plan to tear down its homes. "Crossroads," ruled a committee of the Directorate of Publications (which also censors films), was too one-sided and jeopardized white-black relations, not to mention the international image of South Africa. The committee also complained about the "plaintive voice" of Janet Suzman, the actress who narrated the film. In its 1978 decision the committee offered the film's director, Lindy Wilson, an option. She

12. Interview with Steven McDonald, Pretoria, 26 October 1978.
13. *Sunday Times*, 24 September 1978.

could get it on the air if she changed certain passages. For example, the committee "suggested," instead of maintaining that blacks are heartlessly and arbitrarily being removed from Crossroads, the film should point out that they all have domiciles in the homelands, which is, of course, the Afrikaner notion on which separate development is built.

From the start, SABC promised to apply separate development to television. Officials at Auckland Park say often that the plan for a black television channel, called for in the 1971 government report, has not been abandoned. But deadlines keep getting extended, and few insiders really believe that a second channel will be forthcoming soon. One reason is cost. J. N. Swanepoel, director-general of the SABC, estimates it would cost $232 million to set up. It would require not only an expensive new transmission system but electrification of vast areas as well. Besides, with the white channel working so effectively as the Voice of Pretoria, why risk a black channel? With its daily doses of hard-sell commercials for the good, middle-class life, even state-controlled television raises the expectations of its poorer viewers—the last thing the Nationalists wish to encourage as South Africa's blacks become more and more militant.

For the privilege of being propagandized, South Africans pay the SABC annual tax fees—$9.74 for a radio, $41.76 for a television set. The corporation's 1978 expenditure totaled $155 million, of which $65 million came from these fees. Most of the remainder—$70 million—came from advertising, which began appearing on television at the start of that year. More advertising money was available to television, but SABC limited commercials to 5 percent of the total transmission time. (The 1971 commission report on television recommended an upper limit of 10 percent, and in 1978 would-be advertisers lobbied for an increase to at least 7.5 percent.) The curb on advertising is aimed only partly at keeping commercial glut off the air. It also reflects the concern of the 1971 government report that unbridled commercials on television would lure away advertising from the country's newspapers, so many of which are in shaky financial condition. The SABC, however, has managed to subvert competition in other ways.

As of 1 June 1977 SATV ceased providing complete program information to newspapers. Up to that point daily and weekly papers had been publishing as much as a week's television listings in advance. Now the papers were limited to printing selected highlights. For the full schedule viewers had to purchase one of the SABC weekly magazines, *Family Radio and TV* (in English) or *Radio en TV Dagboek* (in Afrikaans). Besides the listings, the magazines feature advice columns, horoscopes, classic comics, romantic and adventure fiction, and a big dose of puffery under such teasing headlines as "How Jane Seymour Keeps Her Modesty in *'Captains and the Kings.'* " Both periodicals also bulge with advertising, which doubtless pleases Perskor, the Transvaal media conglomerate that prints them.

Newspapers complained bitterly about the 1977 listings embargo, and SABC eventually modified its policy. By late 1978 the papers were again publishing fairly full accounts of upcoming programs—although the SABC still held out on certain shows. The papers sometimes query their bureaus in London or New York for the information. "If there's one thing that tests whether a TV reporter's still got all her marbles," wrote television columnist Gwen Gill, "it's the slog of trying to find out from SATV what's in the pipeline for viewers."[14] For such complaints and other attacks on South African television Gill was banned from SATV's weekly press previews in May 1978.

The SABC also plugged its magazines with four free advertising spots a week, worth an estimated $3.8 million yearly at 1978 rates. These free commercials are stipulated in the 1975 contract between SABC and Perskor, which gets all profits earned by the two magazines into 1985. In return, SABC receives a 3 percent royalty on sales, with a guarantee of $58,000 a year. The cozy arrangement between the SABC and Perskor produces considerable benefits for both. At the end of 1976 *Family Radio and TV* had a circulation of 62,000. By the end of 1977 circulation had risen to 144,000. In the same period *Radio en TV Dagboek*'s circulation jumped from 36,000 to 92,000. These dramatic circulation gains allowed the magazines to jack up their advertising rates—sometimes as much as 100 percent. Given the publication's market and reach, most advertisers were more than willing to pay the increase. They would also be

14. *Sunday Times,* 1 October 1978.

happy to pay the $3.8 million for the free air time SABC dispenses annually to Perskor. But those spots are strictly reserved—the loss absorbed in part by the license fees paid by viewers and listeners.

The SABC-Perskor connection offers a useful illustration of the Nationalist power machine in action, but its significance pales beside the real threat of television, South African style. That comes in the way Auckland Park systematically works on the minds of its daily audience. In the months following the Soweto uprising in 1976, for example, no blacks even remotely critical of the government appeared on television to voice the grievances that led to the unrest and continued to fester. In the hours before the November 1977 general elections, a spokesman for the security police was "interviewed." He attempted to justify Minister of Justice Kruger's crackdown over the preceding months. He talked reassuringly about how violence had declined in the townships since the bannings and detentions of 19 October 1977. He was not asked why Kruger had not brought those he had detained and banned to trial. As one Johannesburg newspaper reporter put it, "with such a powerful and effective propaganda weapon as the SABC, one wonders why the government even bothers to harass the newspapers."[15]

For one reason, it does so because the newspapers—especially the English-language ones—still act as a considerable corrective to television propaganda in South Africa. It was the English-language press, after all, that reported in some detail SABC's refusal to broadcast the Mostert revelations that opened up Muldergate. Nevertheless, television in South Africa, as all over the rest of the globe, is making steady inroads on the influence of print journalism. And to the degree that SATV broadcasts the Big Lie writ large, it provides the government with a powerful weapon with which to neutralize its critics in the press.

15. Interview with reporter who asked not to be identified, Johannesburg, 25 October 1978.

8 The Foreign Bearers of Bad Tidings

On 3 March 1980 the Nationalists seized the passport of Bishop Desmond M. Tutu, general secretary of the South African Council of Churches. But this action, and the implicit threat that a banning order might follow, failed to silence the outspoken black minister, who continued to deliver speeches vehemently attacking the government for its apartheid policy. On May 4 the *New York Times* gave over much of page three to a detailed description of the growing tension between the Nationalists and Tutu. *Times* correspondent John F. Burns reported that Tutu thought the passport seizure was senseless if meant to limit his access to audiences abroad, since his speeches receive wide coverage in the foreign press.

The attitudes and activities of dozens more antiapartheid leaders and organizations also are frequently reported abroad. Moreover, the foreign press corps in South Africa rarely misses major stories that demonstrate the government's repressive nature. The Soweto uprising in 1976, the death of Steve Biko and the bannings and detentions that followed in 1977, and the Muldergate scandal in 1978 and 1979, all drew worldwide coverage, often accompanied by commentary denouncing Nationalist policy.

Government officials smart over the constant assault on their country's image. They regard foreign reporters as second only to members of the domestic English-language press in their capacity to subvert the *Vaderland* and white supremacy. Most Afrikaners think they and their government are completely misunderstood by the outside world. If only the visiting journalist would report South Africa the way the Nationalists see it—as their homeland, to be governed as they please—all would be fine. But the foreign press corps pours out a daily stream of reportage that contradicts at almost every turn the Afrikaner's vision of himself. The correspondents are reporting what they see as the cruel truths of South African life. The Nationalists, however, argue that the outsiders are afflicted with a hopeless bias against their country.

In July 1979 the Information Service of South Africa (ISSA), successor agency to the Department of Information, listed more than eighty journalists as accredited to report for foreign news organizations from South Africa. In addition ISSA's roster included a dozen unaccredited reporters, journalists who dwell in a bureaucratic limbo because the government particularly dislikes their dispatches. Americans and Britons make up almost half the foreign press corps, their numbers roughly evenly divided. The remaining correspondents are primarily European, with a small number from Australia, Japan, and Taiwan, along with a few from South Africa itself. Vlok Delport, the government's liaison with the foreign press, maintained that journalists from black African nations would be considered if they applied for visas.[1] The ISSA roster listed no such correspondents. Reporters from Communist countries need not apply; they are banned by law from entering the country. "The ground rules for getting into South Africa as a foreign journalist," said Delport, "are the most liberal that exist anywhere in the world."[2]

An examination of those ground rules suggests otherwise. To enter South Africa, a reporter must first apply for a visa in his home country. The local South African consulate then sends the application to Pretoria. Most often the government grants the visa, but it is usually good for only three months. During that period the newly arrived correspondent must apply for a multiple reentry visa if he wishes to stay longer. He also must get a work permit and a police press card. The multiple reentry visa must be renewed annually and the work permit every six months. The police bestow—and cancel—the press credentials

1. Interview with Vlok Delport, Pretoria, 26 October 1978.
2. Ibid.

at their pleasure. In addition, in April 1980, a government commission suggested that all correspondents register with the government. William F. Nicholson, Johannesburg bureau chief of the Associated Press and chairman of the sixty-member Foreign Correspondent Association (FCA), found the notion "rather puzzling because there is already a de facto form of registration."[3]

This penchant for overkill in the government's relationship with the foreign press corps dates back to the days when the Nationalists first came to power. The government did not seek to cow only South African newspapers when it established the Press Commission of Inquiry in 1950. The Nationalists called for an examination of the "existing means of self-control and discipline" of "correspondents of overseas newspapers and periodicals and freelance journalists serving the . . . overseas Press."[4] The commission impounded copies of cables filed by correspondents and free-lancers and sifted through thousands of clippings that had appeared in the foreign press. They classified the articles as ranging from "good" to "very bad." Only 6.90 percent qualified as "good," while 47.15 percent were "very bad."[5]

As the Nationalists consolidated power in the 1950s, the "very bad" news flowed steadily out of the country. The foreign press watched apartheid grow increasingly entrenched, especially after H. F. Verwoerd became prime minister in 1958. On 21 March 1960 sixty-nine blacks were killed and more wounded at Sharpeville by police firing into a large crowd protesting the pass laws; the foreign press corps turned the massacre into a symbol of the growing repression of the black majority by the Nationalist minority. The worldwide headlines brought a fury of condemnation down on the Pretoria government, from the United Nations, from other governments, and from leading world citizens.

The government's attitude toward the outside press, which

3. *Rand Daily Mail,* 16 April 1980.
4. *I P I Report,* Monthly Bulletin of the International Press Institute (Zurich: International Press Institute, March 1962), p. 1.
5. Alex Hepple, *Press under Apartheid* (London: International Defense and Aid Fund, 1974). p. 10.

had been stern in the 1950s, now got tougher. *Time* magazine's coverage of Sharpeville and other racial strife so angered the Nationalists that they systematically refused to grant visas to the weekly's would-be correspondents. In 1962 *Time* closed its Johannesburg bureau, relying thereafter largely on a stringer, a British national named Peter Hawthorne. An experienced Africa hand, Hawthorne got his copy out by dictating it over the phone to Salisbury, Rhodesia. There it was put on the wires to Nairobi, Kenya, where *Time*'s bureau sent it on to New York.

Joseph Lelyveld became the *New York Times* correspondent in South Africa in June 1965, just before the *Rand Daily Mail* broke its major exposé of conditions in South Africa's prisons. Not only did Lelyveld write about the *Mail*'s series on prison conditions for the *Times*, he helped arrange for it to be excerpted in the *Times* Sunday magazine (25 July 1965). Those acts, and his subsequent aggressive reporting, angered the authorities. In April 1966 a government official telephoned his wife, Carolyn, while he was on a reporting trip in South West Africa/Namibia. She was told his visa would not be renewed and that his permit to remain in the country would expire in a week. Six days later, Lelyveld flew to London with his family, and the *Times* also closed its bureau.

Besides hectoring correspondents, the government also censored portions of—or banned outright—various foreign publications. The 29 April 1968 issue of *Time* was kept off the stands because it contained an article on Martin Luther King, Jr., that the government deemed objectionable. The 24 December 1969 issue of the *Times* of London carried a special supplement on South Africa and was banned because of advertisements for the International Defence and Aid Fund, Amnesty International, and the Anti-Apartheid Movement. South Africa's newspaper distributors also exercised censorship when they feared the government might take legal action against them. For example, the Central News Agency, the country's largest distributor, deleted an article on the interrogation methods of the South African police before putting the 8 June 1966 issue of Britain's *New Statesman* on sale.

Beginning in the early 1970s, government attitudes toward foreign journalists softened somewhat, at least on the surface.

The Department of Information, with Cornelius Mulder and Eschel Rhoodie then in their ascendancy as minister and secretary, launched a largely cosmetic public relations campaign to win over the outsiders. Selected foreign reporters were invited to a dinner in Pretoria where Mulder, their genial host, promised a new era of cooperation. Then came the first news conference ever held by Prime Minister Vorster. Mulder chaired it and screened all the questions, save a few from the floor at the end of the hour-long session. On several subsequent occasions, groups of foreign correspondents came to Vorster's home for dinner followed by informal, off-the-record background briefings.

Talks even began with *Time* and the *New York Times* about reopening their bureaus in Johannesburg. Initially, Mulder and Rhoodie tried to establish preconditions. For example, they flew to New York and told *Times* executives that reopening its bureau depended on the paper's publishing an article correcting past distortions. Moreover, any new correspondent faced a six-month trial period and the *Times* must agree that if he wrote anything that displeased the South African government no publicity would be given his deportation. The *Times* declined the conditions but did agree to consider and subsequently published an article on the Afrikaner point of view. (It appeared in the *New York Sunday Times Magazine* of 12 December 1976 under the byline of P. J. Cillie, former editor of *Die Burger*.)

Rather than immediately reopen its bureau in Johannesburg, the *Times* sent reporter Charles Mohr on a temporary assignment in 1975. Over a six-month period Mohr toured the country and wrote a series of solid, frank articles about many aspects of South African society, black and white. Rhoodie did not like all of them, but he conceded that Mohr had gotten his facts right. Just before Mohr's visa expired, he lunched with Rhoodie and Mulder in Pretoria; they told him he could become the *Times*'s permanent correspondent. Mohr, who had covered the war in Southeast Asia, had an adopted Vietnamese daughter. When he asked if he could bring her to live with him, Mulder replied: "No, I regret that will not be possible."[6]

6. "How Eschel Rhoodie Fought the Paper Curtain," *Capetonian*, February 1979, p. 9.

The Foreign Bearers of Bad Tidings

In May 1976 John Burns became the *Times*'s first permanent correspondent in South Africa since Lelyveld was expelled ten years earlier. While covering a session of Parliament in Cape Town, he introduced himself to Prime Minister Vorster, saying he had come to observe all aspects of the country and to write fairly. "Vorster was a block of stone," Burns recalled. "As I spoke, he raised his hand, cut me off, and said, 'If you do not know now you will soon learn that I am a very blunt man. I do not like your newspaper. And may I remind you that your predecessor did not stay very long.' "[7]

A month after Burns arrived Soweto exploded. He and his fellow correspondents poured out copy that vividly depicted the inhuman conditions in the townships. With its reportorial consciousness steadily rising in the weeks that followed, the foreign press corps began filing dispatches that further tarnished South Africa's image. They infuriated the government and, not surprisingly, the public relations honeymoon initiated by the Department of Information ended. The government threw no correspondents out of the country, as Vorster had suggested might happen to Burns if he did not toe the line. But Mulder and Rhoodie went back on the offensive, often by seeking equal time in a correspondent's newspaper or by trying to manipulate coverage by going directly to his or her boss.

For example, in January 1977, the *Washington Post* ran a series of articles on South Africa by Jim Hoagland, a Pulitzer Prize-winning reporter. The articles so incensed Rhoodie that when the *Post* refused to give him enough space to reply, the Department of Information answered with a three-quarter page advertisement on April 24. Rhoodie had better luck with the *International Herald Tribune* in Paris. It ran his attack as an article on April 18. Two days later Hoagland responded with a letter calling the article "totally frivolous" and concluding that "a trouble-maker intent on satirizing or discrediting Mr. Rhoodie has obtained the secretary's letterhead stationery and perpetrated a hoax on your readers."

For years the South African government refused to grant a visa to any American correspondent from *Newsweek*, which is owned by the Washington Post Company. The Department of

7. Interview with John F. Burns, Johannesburg, 2 November 1978.

Information claimed that the newsmagazine consistently had indulged an anti-Nationalist bias.[8] "If you examine the back bench of *Newsweek*, you'll probably find a black man or a communist there," Rhoodie told Peter Younghusband, a South African citizen who served as the weekly's bureau chief in Cape Town.[9]

In the eyes of the government, a white countryman sending "negative" information abroad approaches the ultimate treason. Rhoodie denied Younghusband official accreditation as a foreign correspondent. But the reporter had developed his own access to Nationalist leaders and other sources over the years, and his stories kept appearing in *Newsweek*. In the mid-1970s Rhoodie began attacking the articles in letters and telexes to *Newsweek* in New York, at one point demanding that Younghusband be fired for reporting alleged historical inaccuracies.[10] On one occasion, *Newsweek* received such a heated telex about Younghusband's reporting that the editors asked their correspondent to call Rhoodie and make sure he had really sent it. "Yes, it was me who sent it—and it should have been stronger," Rhoodie yelled over the telephone.[11]

Rhoodie and others in the Department of Information harassed Paul Schumacher a good deal, too. They loathed the stinging dispatches he filed for *Der Spiegel*, the West German newsweekly. But Schumacher, a West German national who had lived in Pretoria for a number of years, had a South African passport; he did not need a visa to enter the country to operate as *Der Spiegel*'s full-time correspondent. Like *Newsweek*'s Younghusband, he failed to get official accreditation despite repeated requests to the information department. "They didn't like my point of view," Schumacher recalled.[12]

Der Spiegel regularly featured interviews with foreign leaders. Rhoodie suggested to Schumacher that he might get accredited if Rhoodie himself were interviewed. Schumacher was told that he would not have to do any work; the Department of

8. "How Eschel Rhoodie Fought the Paper Curtain," p. 9.
9. Ibid.
10. Ibid., p. 11.
11. Ibid.
12. Interview with Paul Schumacher, Pretoria, 26 October 1978.

Information was prepared to furnish the whole exercise—questions and answers. Schumacher declined and *Der Spiegel* persuaded the Bonn government to lodge a protest with Pretoria over the interference with its correspondent.

Schumacher went about his business, arranging through his private contacts to conduct an interview with R. F. (Pik) Botha, minister of foreign affairs. In May 1978 press officer Delport urgently summoned Schumacher to the Department of Information. Delport castigated the correspondent for not setting up the interview through the department. Ignoring the fact that Botha had agreed to participate, Delport told Schumacher that "there is no way you will do an interview with Pik until you've done one with Rhoodie."[13] Schumacher said he was prepared to interview Rhoodie if tough questioning were allowed.

Schumacher called Rhoodie numerous times to arrange a date, but he received no response. Finally, he went back to Delport to ask for help. Instead of calling Rhoodie, Delport reached into his desk drawer and produced a neatly typewritten interview. Schumacher read it and was stunned. "It was great," he recalled. "There was some propaganda, of course, but it was full of good, critical questions, just as I might have asked them. And the whole thing was set up just as *Der Spiegel* would have done it."[14] The magazine did not run the "interview." By this time Muldergate was in full cry and Rhoodie soon fell from grace. Once that happened, Schumacher got his interview with Pik Botha—but not his accreditation.

While the Department of Information pursued such Marx Brothers manipulation, South African security operatives kept tabs on the foreign press by more routine police-state methods. Most correspondents assume their telephones are tapped and have frequent evidence. In May 1979, for example, Caryl Murphy of the *Washington Post* received a call in Johannesburg from Millard Arnold of the Lawyers Committee for Equal Rights in South Africa. Arnold was calling from Windhoek, capital of South West Africa/Namibia; he had information about troop movements and political developments in that territory, in

13. Ibid.
14. Ibid.

which South Africa has a vital interest. When Arnold got down to specifics, the telephone went dead.[15]

In February 1978 Murphy flew to East London on a reporting trip. When she arrived at her hotel, the receptionist told her the police had come to check on her arrival. Soon after Murphy started out on her assignment in a rented car she realized she was being followed. She stopped the car, got out, and the following exchange took place with her South African police shadow:

"Do you plan to follow me all day?"

"It looks like it."

"How did you know I was here?"

"Oh, like the Russians, we have our ways and means."[16]

Port Elizabeth is the center of black radicalism in South Africa. The banned African National Congress was founded there and Steve Biko was detained and beaten there in 1977. When June Goodwin of the *Christian Science Monitor* flew down from Johannesburg to investigate conditions in Port Elizabeth she was trailed everywhere by the police. Even as she was leaving, the police kept at it. At the airport she was told by a local reporter that the head of the security police had called him to say that if he happened to be looking for Goodwin she was just leaving. "It was sheer intimidation," she recalled.[17] More intimidation followed from Washington: South African Ambassador D. B. Sole wrote to the *Monitor*'s editor, suggesting that Goodwin faced expulsion if her unflattering articles continued. But Goodwin kept sending out reports that embarrassed and angered the Nationalists, and the *Monitor* kept printing them.

The government did not make good its threat to throw her out. Like many other correspondents covering South Africa in the 1970s, she had a certain immunity because she worked for a well-known news organization. The Nationalists disliked her dispatches, but they liked even less the publicity sure to flare up worldwide if they expelled her or any of her peers. Such antidemocratic behavior would smack of the Soviet Union, and

15. Interview with Caryl Murphy, Johannesburg, 21 May 1979.
16. Ibid.
17. Interview with June Goodwin, Johannesburg, 17 October 1978.

The Foreign Bearers of Bad Tidings

the Afrikaner leaders do not relish inviting that comparison—
however willing a security minion might be to do so.

Fairer game for the government, however, are the stringers
and other less visible free-lancers who scramble for stories on
an *ad hoc* basis, often for more than one foreign news outlet. In
1977 Daniel Drooz was stringing for both the *Chicago Sun-Times*
and *Maariv*, the Israeli daily. At a dinner party for foreign correspondents, a government official accused Drooz, an American, of spying for both the Central Intelligence Agency and the
Israelis. In July he was given nine days to leave the country,
only to have the order rescinded as suddenly as it had mate-
rialized. The following year, however, the government struck
again, telling Drooz to get out by August 31. Nelson Harvey,
deputy U.S. Ambassador in Pretoria, protested to Foreign
Minister Pik Botha, seeking at the least an explanation for the
expulsion. He got none. The *Sun-Times* sought help from South
African Ambassador Sole in Washington. But these bureaucratic maneuvers came only days before the deadline; by August 31 Drooz had left the country.

Technically the government can detain a foreign journalist
without charge for allegedly breaking one or more of the many
antipress laws enacted by the Nationalists over the years. Detention seldom takes place, for the same reason reporters only
rarely get thrown out of the country—the government's concern
for its image. But exceptions occasionally occur. In April 1979
Ole Eriksen, a Norwegian reporter and a representative of the
International Federation of Journalists, was detained and interrogated for two hours by the Johannesburg police. He had held
discussions in Soweto with a group of nonwhite journalists, six
of whom were detained with him. The police brought no
charges against Eriksen, who held a valid permit to visit Soweto. In 1977 a correspondent for a major U.S. daily was
threatened with a contempt of court citation for his coverage of
Steve Biko's death at the hands of the police and related events
that followed. The charge carried a two-year prison penalty.
The reporter (who asked not to be identified) never seriously
feared he would be imprisoned, but he thought the government
might bring the charge and then expel him. Ultimately, dip-

lomatic channels were used to calm down the Nationalists, and the correspondent remained in South Africa.

Most journalists who seek entry to South Africa on a temporary basis receive relatively cordial treatment and little harassment. Unlike resident correspondents, those who come in on special assignments tend to be unknown quantities. The government seems to assume—or at least hope—that these journalists are not afflicted with an anti-Nationalist bias. For example, the government proved cooperative in helping NBC correspondent Garrick Utley and his crew film around the country in early 1977. "They go through periods when they try to portray themselves as good guys, and this was apparrently one of them," Utley recalled. "The government was concerned about Carter's human rights onslaught."[18]

The Nationalists even agreed to let additional NBC staff into the country to produce a documentary. Utley and the unit operated relatively unfettered. They reported on and filmed South African troops stationed at the Angolan border. They descended into a gold mine and interviewed black miners. They shot footage at a Johannesburg labor exchange, where blacks line up in a desperate search for work. And they had access to Soweto to film as they wished. "There were few limitations that I could see," said Utley, "although I assume we were watched most of the time."[19]

Certainly the documentary was watched by South African diplomats in the United States when it aired in July 1977. Called "Africa's Defiant White Tribe," it sought to give an even-handed portrait of contemporary South Africa. But, as always, the facts and arithmetic of the country's racist society produced a fairly unflattering picture of Afrikanerdom. In particular, the Nationalists objected to the Transvaal farmer NBC chose as one voice of the white tribe. "He was like a Cook County ward heeler," Utley recalled. "He spoke his mind. And one of the things he said was that God didn't create all men equal."[20] The Nationalists struck back at NBC by showing some of the footage on SABC television with sections taken out of context. They

18. Interview with Garrick Utley, New York, 3 May 1980.
19. Ibid.
20. Ibid.

offered this bowdlerized version as an example of how the foreign media distorted the truth about South Africa. Mulder himself presided over this television propaganda.

The Nationalists' deep suspicion of the foreign journalists is heightened by the fact that virtually none of them speaks or understands Afrikaans. When foreign correspondents interview government leaders, the give-and-take almost always occurs in English, the language most Afrikaner leaders still regard disdainfully as the tongue of the imperialist interloper. Some correspondents subscribe to a translation service that gives them a daily précis of the Afrikaans-language newspapers. But most use the antigovernment English-language press as their major source for stories. Moreover, many correspondents gravitate toward the Nationalist-baiting *Rand Daily Mail,* which in the eyes of the government leaders proves more than anything else the innate anti-Afrikaner bias of the foreign journalist.

The constant war of nerves between the Nationalists and the foreign press corps inevitably produces a certain chilling effect. Though the flow of news out of South Africa is indisputably negative, many dispatches lack the critical edge they might have in a freer society. Correspondents know that to come down too hard too often courts expulsion. Many foreign journalists also stick safely with the pack, filing whatever story might be "hot" at the moment. Only a very few regularly venture into the townships or homelands and risk an almost certain collision with the unpredictable security police. "There is also the problem of self-censorship," admitted one correspondent. "A good deal of it goes on all the time, no doubt about it."[21]

That, of course, is among the occupational hazards of being a foreign correspondent in many nations. So are carefully calculated bureaucratic obstacles like visas, work permits, and police credentials, as well as tapped phones, security sleuths, and harassment in general. South Africa's treatment of visiting journalists may not be quite as "liberal" as press officer Delport insists, but it is as good as many countries and better than many more. The Soviet Union and the Warsaw Pact countries are much quicker to expel aggressive foreign correspondents

21. Interview with a correspondent who asked not to be identified, Johannesburg, 2 November 1978.

and place much more of their territory off limits than South Africa does. The majority of governments—Communist and non-Communist—in Asia, black Africa, the Middle East, and Latin America create atmospheres far more hostile to foreign journalists than Pretoria—and often more physically dangerous as well.

The International Press Institute's "World Press Freedom Review of 1979" records no acts of violence against foreign correspondents in South Africa. However: in Uganda soldiers loyal to President Amin murdered four West German journalists in cold blood; in Zambia an Australian television reporter was critically wounded by government troops; in Nicaragua National Guardsmen shot dead at point blank range an American television journalist; in Pakistan a British reporter described by the government as a snooper was beaten up in the street.

The Nationalists' *relatively* benign attitude toward foreign journalists reflects, once again, the Afrikaner's abiding belief in the idea of white democracy. The foreign press corps is white, thus for all its hostility it must be treated with the basic respect reserved for all whites in South Africa's apartheid culture. To treat the foreign press corps with true severity, or to greatly limit the number of correspondents in the country, would be to admit that South Africa is not the open society the Nationalists claim it to be. As the ironic result, the bad news continues to flow abroad, the country's image worsens, and the Afrikaner persists in the notion that the outside world fails to understand him.

9 The Future

The South African government moved into the 1980s pointing proudly to developments it claimed demonstrated a sincere commitment to a better life for blacks. "We must adapt or die," Prime Minister Botha said repeatedly, as he traveled the country talking reform.[1] He even ventured into Soweto and told a black audience, "We are all South Africans."[2] To back up these words, the Nationalists further reduced petty apartheid restrictions and introduced some mild labor reforms. In addition, Botha announced that the government was exploring the possibility of ending the ban on interracial marriages and of providing more land for the homeland territories. On a visit to the United States in June 1979, Dr. Pieter Koornhof, South Africa's minister of cooperation and development, assured the National Press Club in Washington that his country had reached "a turning point in our history. Apartheid, as you came to know it in the United States, is dying and dead."[3]

Even the most embittered blacks concede that the government seemed genuinely determined to at least modify its historic hard line. But not in any truly meaningful way. "If apartheid is dead," said Percy Qoboza, "then urgent funeral arrangements need to be made because the body is still around and it is making a terrible smell."[4] Bishop Desmond Tutu, secretary general of the South African Council of Churches, argued

1. *New York Times,* 22 November 1979.
2. Ibid., 28 October 1979.
3. Aryeh Neier, "Selling Apartheid," *Nation,* 11–18 August 1979, p. 104.
4. *New York Times,* 28 October 1979.

that Botha sought to apply "an inhumane system more humanely. . . . There has been no fundamental change."[5]

By "no fundamental change," Bishop Tutu and most other critics of the government refer to the homeland policy. Whatever additional land *might* be forthcoming from Pretoria, the Nationalists remained totally committed to "separate development." On 13 September 1979, three months after Koornhof pronounced apartheid dead in Washington, South Africa bestowed "independence" on the 320,000 natives of Venda, an area about half the size of Connecticut at the Zimbabwe border. This destitute new "nation"—per capita income $26 a month—is the third homeland to achieve "independence" after the Transkei (1976) and Bophuthatswana (1977). The international community rejects this charade, refusing to grant these enclaves diplomatic recognition, but Pretoria relentlessly plays its denationalization game nonetheless.

Most Afrikaners fully embrace the homeland policy. They insist that once all ten homelands are independent ("independenced" might be a better word), apartheid will, indeed, be dead. The black tribes will have their own nations, their own governments, their own destiny. Never mind that they will have had no say in the matter, that the whites will have retained by far the most and best of the country, that the homelands are at once impoverished and economically bound to the white business nexus, and that millions of blacks will continue to live outside their so-called homelands—in the appalling urban townships—so they can earn a living by serving the white boss.

The cruel deception of the Nationalists' cosmetic reforms drew increasing anger and protest from the nonwhite community as the 1980s began. Strikes, school boycotts, and random attacks on police stations rose dramatically. Black guerrillas showed a new boldness as well. In January 1980 three members of the long-banned African National Congress raided a bank in the Pretoria suburb of Silverton; they took twenty-five hostages and demanded the release of imprisoned ANC leader Nelson Mandela. Six months later, on June 1, the ANC firebombed three major South African oil complexes, causing an estimated $8 million in damage.

5. Ibid., 22 November 1979.

As always in the past, the government's reaction was swift and stern. In mid-1980 alone, some thirty nonwhites died at the hands of the police while protesting inferior education in the Cape Province. (Exactly how many died, and in precisely what circumstances, were impossible to determine because journalists were barred from the townships and any other place police official regarded as "operational areas.")[6] All three guerrillas who took over the bank near Pretoria were killed by police; two hostages died in the cross fire and ten more were wounded. A crowd estimated at some twenty thousand people, mostly students, attended the funeral of one of the guerrillas, Fannie Mafoko, a former leader of the Soweto Students' Representative Council. As the gathering marched from the cemetery and through Soweto, police charged in and fired tear gas. The saboteurs who hit the oil installations were not immediately caught. But their success served mainly to tighten security nationwide.

The headlines produced by the growing violence between whites and nonwhites sometimes suggest that South Africa has entered a true state of revolutionary collision. But it is a mistake to make too much of these isolated clashes. For all its numerical strength and growing sense of desperation, the nonwhite majority remains seriously fragmented politically. Despite years of efforts, neither the black leadership inside the country nor in the exile community has been able to agree on a united front against the Afrikaner.

Meanwhile, the Nationalists' solidarity has only increased and is backed up by a fierce war machine. At 8,500 regulars, South Africa's standing army is small. But most young men must put in two years of national service, giving the country a call-up reserve of 404,500, virtually all white. "These forces," noted the *Economist*, "are almost double the total combined strengths of South Africa's seven immediate black neighbours, many of whose armies are ill-equipped and of doubtful military effectiveness."[7] Add the irony that these same black states, whatever their politics and public condemnations of the

6. *South Africa/Namibia Update*, 2 July 1980.
7. Simon Jenkins, "The Great Evasion—South Africa: A survey," *The Economist*, 21 June 1980, p. 24.

Afrikaners, are increasingly dependent on the Nationalists economically, and the immediate prospect for South Africa's non-whites looks gloomy indeed.

Almost without exception, South Africa's journalists view the 1980s with a deep foreboding—both for their nation and for themselves. Nor, in the end, does their triumphant role in exposing the information scandal encourage them much. For all the headlines, Muldergate reduces to an affair of the till in the eyes of most Afrikaners. Eschel Rhoodie sinned because he made off with the swag, not because he and Cornelius Mulder devised a worldwide propaganda plan to justify and sell South Africa's racial policies. This is not to minimize the press's role in Muldergate, which was central and courageous. But it would be a serious mistake to conclude that the exposé, and all the sound and fury that accompanied it, signaled any fundamental political change in South Africa.

The government appears more determined than ever to pursue separate development, at the same time increasing the pressure on its critics in the press. Prime Minister Botha's post-Muldergate legislation, which put four new major press curbs on the books, is merely one example. Another example is the sentencing in August 1979 of Zwelahke Sisulu, news editor of the *Sunday Post,* to nine months in prison for refusing to testify against one of his reporters, Thami Mkhwanazi, who had been detained the month before under the Terrorism Act. In a rare admission, police conceded they had tapped the two journalists' phone conversations.

Sisulu's plight reflects much more than simply the collision between press and state in South Africa. Early in 1979 he and two other reporters moved from the *Rand Daily Mail* to the *Post.* They felt the *Mail* increasingly pulled its punches in the face of escalating government pressure. Hardly a journalist in South Africa, whatever his politics or color, would deny the charge, nor limit it to the *Mail.* The white press entered the 1980s in an extracautious mood. Understandably, black journalists regard the coming decade as a time not for retrenchment but for progress, however tough and hazardous the going. Sisulu's and his colleagues' departure from the *Mail* illustrates a growing polarization between black and white journalists just when they need each other most. This split mirrors the widening chasm in the society at large. On 12 March 1978 at the funeral of Robert Sobukwe, militant black youths angrily demanded that the Pan-Africanist Congress president not be eulogized with speeches by white liberals or moderate blacks. They persuaded the Sobukwe family to purge the original list of speakers of, among others, Benjamin Pogrund, deputy editor of the *Rand Daily Mail*.

Pogrund is the classic, liberal, English-speaking, white South African newspaperman. He has fought apartheid and other government injustice since joining the *Mail* in 1958. For his efforts, he has won the respect and praise of many of his colleagues, inside the country and outside; he has been to jail, threatened with more incarceration, had his passport revoked, and faced almost constant harassment over the years. Like many of his white compatriots with similar views and histories, he is weary of the struggle. "Remember," says one, "we have been preaching now for more than thirty years, and things have gotten worse not better."[8] Moreover, South Africa's liberal press now finds itself increasingly castigated by militant blacks for softheadedness at best and caving in at worst. Trapped between rising black anger on the left and Afrikaner repression on the right, the liberal journalist occupies narrower ground with every passing year.

During the denouement of Muldergate it looked as if the Afrikaans-language press, angered by the Nationalists' thirst for legislative revenge over the information scandal revelations, might at last close ranks with the English-language press. The two camps did make common cause against the section of the Advocate-General Bill that would have made it a crime to publish articles about corruption without first getting the government's permission. Pressure from the Nationalist press indisputably played a major role in the defeat of that provision. Even the staff association of the SABC denounced the restriction. And young reporters at *Beeld* were so furious over their party's antipress rampage they sought to have their paper

8. Interview with Martin Schneider, Johannesburg, 25 October 1978.

withdraw its support for a Nationalist candidate in a local by-election.

But calmer Afrikaner heads prevailed. J. N. Swanepoel, director-general of SABC, immediately repudiated his staff's protest and assured the government that the vast majority of the network was loyal. In an editorial, *Beeld*'s "more experienced men" rejected the idea of staying out of the by-election. "[T]here is more to it than personalities. There is the future of South Africa and the future of Afrikanerdom. . . . The elemental truth is that the party cannot achieve its tasks without its Press, or the Press without its party."[9] However strongly the Afrikner journalist may feel occasionally about the antipress excesses of his government, he remains locked in a system that offers almost no chance of escape to independence.

"We have a feeling of inevitability," says Martin Schneider, political editor of the *Rand Daily Mail*. "A lot of the more idealistic guys have left. They feel there's no more sense in being around. The *Mail* used to be a much tougher paper, far more outspoken."[10] However, Allister Sparks, the paper's editor, vows to "struggle on, as we have before, and try to be as effective as we can."[11] Sparks sees the liberal press as an agency for peaceful change, which may seem hopelessly optimistic in the increasingly polarized atmosphere of South Africa today. But should the English-language press grow fainter—either as a result of more government restrictions or as a further collapse of journalistic will—conditions are hardly likely to improve. Whatever its shortcomings, however frightened it appears to the blacks, the English-language newspapers remain a pivotal force in trying to head off a catastrophe in South Africa. How long they will be able to hang on in their present precarious position is impossible to estimate. One can only hope, with Benjamin Pogrund, "that the lingering emphasis on democracy in this curious country" will somehow continue to provide enough oxygen to sustain the men and women of the South African press.[12]

The international journalistic community has not yet found

9. *Beeld*, 19 May 1979.
10. Interview with Martin Schneider, Johannesburg, 25 October 1978.
11. Interview with Allister Sparks, Johannesburg, 22 May 1979.
12. Interview with Benjamin Pogrund, Johannesburg, 16 May 1979.

a concrete way to help its South African colleagues. The problem is not one of indifference. Western news organizations, and individual journalists (including correspondents based in South Africa), almost ritually decry the plight of the South African press. The International Press Institute in London registers formal protests, Amnesty International and the *Index on Censorship* chart the bannings and detentions. The Newspaper Guild sends an observer to the trials of journalists and contributes money to their defense. All this is important, but considering the size of the problem, it hardly makes a dent. And it gets the Nationalists' backs up even further.

When specific aid is offered, it may become a terrible two-edged sword, as the experience of the Nieman Foundation demonstrates. Established in 1938, the foundation's program offers selected American and foreign journalists a chance to study anything they want for an academic year at Harvard University. Beginning in the early 1960s a South African journalist entered the program every year. The South African selection committee sent an Afrikaner one year, an Englisher the next. In 1972 James C. Thomson, Jr., became the new Nieman curator, and two years later he announced he would end the program's relationship with South Africa unless black journalists began arriving in Cambridge. For the 1975–76 academic year the selection committee sent Percy Qoboza.

Qoboza returned to South Africa a politically sensitized and far tougher editor. As a result, his *World* and *Weekend World* became much more trenchant—for which they were closed and Qoboza jailed on 19 October 1977. "In one sense," says Thomson, "we might have done better to leave Percy and other black journalists be. The consciousness-raising at Harvard is exhilarating, but it's also terrifying. Percy left his kids behind, for example; if you leave kids back there they become hostages." Moreover, he adds, the black South African fellows "go through the torture of the damned because they get involved with the exile community and are surrounded by people fighting from the outside. Still, there is an extraordinary love of country, and they want to go back and fight for their people."[13]

13. Interview with James C. Thomson, Jr., Cambridge, Mass., 18 September 1979.

When Qoboza went to prison, the Nieman Foundation served as a clearinghouse for the worldwide outcry over his fate. Late in 1977 Thomson led a delegation of Neiman fellows to Washington for a meeting with South Africa's ambassador to the United States, D. B. Sole. Thomson recalls that at one point in the hour-and-a-half session, Sole assured them that Qoboza was "in good condition in a very safe and respectable prison."[14] When one of the fellows asked which prison, Sole sheepishly conceded he did not in fact know. Nor did the information officer sitting in on the meeting. The ambassador offered the services of his diplomatic pouch so the fellows could correspond with Qoboza, but Thomson said their letters never made it to Qoboza's cell.

The hazards of programs that bring black South African journalists into the heady atmosphere of free thought and association are clear. When they go back into the political smog of their country, they will choke more than ever. In the end, though, moral support, for all its seeming ineffectiveness, may be the only way to keep the pressure on the Nationalists. "It would be terribly demoralizing if our colleagues abroad stopped supporting us," says the *Mail*'s Sparks. "It's one of the few things that keep us going."[15]

14. Ibid.
15. Interview with Allister Sparks, Johannesburg, 22 May 1979.

98

Appendixes

Index

Introduction to Appendixes

On 3 November 1978 Prime Minister P. W. Botha appointed a Commission of Inquiry into Alleged Irregularities in the former Department of Information. It consisted of George Frederik Smalberger, chief state law adviser; Abraham Jacobus Lategan, attorney general of the Cape Province; and Rudolf Philip Botha Erasmus, judge of the Free State Provincial Division of the Supreme Court. Erasmus was named chairman, and the body quickly became known as the Erasmus commission. The commission, which heard witnesses in camera and collected more than eleven thousand pages of evidence and testimony, issued three reports: the first on 6 December 1978, the second on 31 March 1979, and the last on 30 May 1979.

In all, the reports afford a rare look at the worldwide propaganda manipulations of the South African government and the corruption that accompanied them. Unfortunately, space limitations prohibit recording the Erasmus findings in their entirety. What follows then are two of the most telling portions of the reports. The first (Appendix A) deals with "Project Annemarie," the establishment of a pro-Nationalist, English-language daily, the *Citizen*, with millions of rands in secret government funds. Appendix A consists of chapter nine of the December report and chapter three of the May report. Appendix B, which consists of chapter ten of the May report, explores the clandestine efforts of the information department to help Michigan publisher John McGoff buy the *Washington Star* with government money. Both appendixes should be read in the context provided by chapter three of this book.

Introduction

The Erasmus commission published most of its findings in English. Those passages in Afrikaans—primarily quoted testimony—have been translated and are bracketed. For reference purposes, each paragraph begins with a number. Throughout the text, citations occasionally occur in roman or arabic numerals. For the most part, these refer to the volumes of evidence collected by the commission or to a section of one of the three reports. Most of the people discussed in the appendixes have previously appeared in this book. However, for the reader who wishes to refresh his memory, a list of the dramatis personae follows:

ALBERTS, J. VAN Z., publisher of *To the Point*, a weekly propaganda magazine secretly supported by the government, and one of the Department of Information's chief front men;

BARRIE, P. G., retired auditor-general of South Africa who conducted an early audit inspection of the Department of Information that uncovered considerable irregularities;

DE VILLIERS, L. E. S., a key operative of the Department of Information, especially in Washington, D.C.;

DIEDERICHS, NICOLAAS, South Africa's state president from 1975 until his death in 1978;

DU PREEZ, P. F., one of Louis Luyt's accountants;

FOURIE, BRAAM, an accountant with the Department of Information;

GRAAFF, DEVILLIERS, former leader of the United party whom Eschel Rhoodie drew into the information department's aborted attempt to buy South African Associated Newspapers with government funds;

HORWOOD, OWEN, South Africa's finance minister;

JONES, VIC, a business associate of John McGoff's;

JUSSEN, HUBERT G., founder of *To the Point*;

LUYT, LOUIS, the fertilizer magnate who fronted as "owner" of the *Citizen*;

McGOFF, JOHN, Michigan publisher and friend of South African government officials, among them Cornelius Mulder and Eschel Rhoodie;

MULDER, CORNELIUS, minister of information;

REYNDERS, L. S., a Nationalist bureaucrat who undertook an

102

investigation of the Department of Information only to find out too much and have his life threatened;

RHOODIE, D. O., Eschel Rhoodie's brother and an employee of the information department;

RHOODIE, ESCHEL, Secretary of Information and architect of the secret information war;

SPRINGER, AXEL, West German communications magnate;

VAN DEN BERGH, HENDRIK, former head of the Bureau for State Security and key behind-the-scenes manipulator in the Muldergate scandal;

VAN ROOYEN, RETIEF, a lawyer who served as a director of Thor Communicators, a Department of Information front, and who was among the first to help expose the department;

VORSTER, B. J., prime minister and then state president of South Africa until forced to resign in 1979 because of his role in the information scandal.

Appendix A: The *Citizen*

9.226 In order to determine how this particular secret project of the Department originated the Commission had to consider the evidence of, in particular, Mr. Vorster, Dr. Mulder, Dr. Rhoodie, Van den Bergh and Alberts, and all available documentation.

9.227 Dr. Mulder and Dr. Rhoodie, backed up to a large extent by Alberts, testified that as early as the beginning of 1973 a conviction had been growing in their minds that tremendous harm was being done to the RSA [Republic of South Africa] by reporting and comment in the South African English-language newspapers which presented a selective image of RSA to the world. In their view this was a distorted and incorrect image and a method had to be found of placing the true objective picture in perspective for those who had access to press reports and comment only through the medium of English.

9.228 In their evidence before the Commission they pointed out that thousands of immigrants and tourists, among others, entered South Africa every year and that they were almost totally dependent on the English language newspapers for an evaluation of the South African situation.

9.229 To sum up, their view was (and is) that there were virtually only two alternatives to counter these problems, either press censorship or the establishment of an English language daily newspaper which would as far as possible present the objective facts to English-speakers independently. Dr. Mulder's view may therefore be summed up more or less as being that the eventual cost to the State of the *Citizen* was in a sense the price South Africa had to pay to avoid press censorship.

9.230 With this idea uppermost, they further saw it as the task of the Department to put the picture in the correct perspective. A start was made early in 1973 with an attempt to take over the *Natal Mercury* with the assistance of a certain Mr. Morgan. According to Dr. Rhoodie, Dr. Piet Koornhof, one of your Cabinet Ministers, Mr. Morgan and Van den Bergh explored the idea. However, nothing came of it.

9.231 According to Dr. Rhoodie, the idea was to gain control of South African Associated Newspapers, hereinafter referred to as SAAN. The idea was put forward for the first time by Alberts at a [barbecue] at Van den Bergh's home during the winter of 1975. Because Dr. Rhoodie thought it a good idea he discussed it shortly afterwards with Dr. Mulder, who signified his agreement.

9.232 At that stage the SAAN shares were dropping sharply and it was thought that it was a golden opportunity of obtaining control at a reasonable price of one of the most powerful groups of English-language publications in the RSA. It was realized right from the start by all concerned that such a takeover would not be possible without the use of funds from the Exchequer.

9.233 Alberts, who had formerly held an executive position in the Rentmeester group of companies, was at this stage already being employed by the Department's secret fund at a remuneration of R15,000 per annum (tax-free) to act as an agent, or front, for the Department in the carrying out of secret projects.

9.234 As a proven businessman, and also as a chartered accountant, he was well equipped to handle the financial interests of the secret project outwardly, and, with his knowledge of the share market, he saw the opportunity of taking over SAAN.

9.235 It had also come to his knowledge that the heirs of the Bailey Trust, who held the key shares in SAAN, were dissatisfied with the dividends they were receiving from their shares at that stage.

9.236 According to his own evidence, Dr. Mulder was closely involved in the take-over plan from the start. According to him and Dr. Rhoodie, Mr. Vorster was also kept informed of the plan and the way in which it would be carried out. Dr. Rhoodie alleges that he informed Mr. Vorster that, if the take-over of SAAN did not succeed, steps would be proceeded with to start an English-language newspaper of its own with the Department's funds. According to Dr. Rhoodie, Mr. Vorster's reaction to this was that it was all right, but that ["you must take care not to catch your coat in the door."]

9.237 Later in this report the Commission will revert to and deal fully with Mr. Vorster's knowledge of the planning and execution of a project by the Department to control English-language newspapers, or alternatively a newspaper, with funds from the Exchequer.

9.238 Shortly after Dr. Rhoodie's discussion with Dr. Mulder, referred to above, the former told Dr. Mulder, in the presence of Van den Bergh, that Alberts required R200,000 to buy a block of SAAN shares and that ["the matter has been approved."] The amount was provided from the secret fund with Dr. Mulder's approval and Alberts bought the available shares. Project Annemarie had commenced.

9.239 Dr. Mulder accounts for his action in attempting to take over SAAN and subsequently establishing the *Citizen* on the strength of a letter from Mr. Vorster in December 1973 to the Ministers of Finance, Defense, Foreign Affairs, Bantu Administration, Economic Affairs, Police, Mines, Immigration and Sport and Recreation. Under the title: ["Responsibilities and Duties of the Overseas Information Department."]

This letter read as follows:

["In view of the increasing political and propaganda attacks on this republic, in both intensity and extent, in addition to their false and perverted form, it has become necessary to adapt the functions of the Information Department to the promotion of our country's interests in general and to national security in particular accordingly. This situation further sets new standards for the department to devise suitable ways and means for the purpose.

"This instruction to the Information Department and the task set for it overseas is to communicate by all possible means to the people of other countries, especially to their leaders of public opinion and decision makers in all fields, government policies already announced together with all relevant facts concerning this republic and Southwest Africa. This order proceeds from the presidential notice of the establishment of the Information Department. In that presidential proclamation, included in governmental decree No. 1142 of December 1, 1961, the provision of information over public reports and rumors from South Africa and Southwest Africa and their evolution to the populations of South Africa and other countries were entrusted to the Information Department (paragraphs b and c), together with the domestic and overseas coordination of all of the government publicity services (paragraph d), the performance of all incidental services, and information on all aspects of the manner of living and activities of South Africa to be distributed (paragraph e and paragraph f) and performance of such functions as may be resolved upon from time to time.

"The execution of this order by the department, the realization of its objective, the methods to be employed, as also the financing of all actions form part of the titular responsibilities of the Minister of Information in consultation with the Secretary of State for Foreign Affairs. In the performance of his instructions, it is left to the Minister of Information to define which methods, means, and activities, whether public or secret, will be needful and most effective for the accomplishment of the above-mentioned objectives.

"The Minister of Information, to consult on the nature of the matter with the Prime Minister as to important informational aspects and projects, shall follow cabinet guidance on those matters which may require cabinet consideration and concern."]

9.240 In this regard Dr. Mulder also referred to Government Notice No. 1142, dated 1 December 1961, paragraphs (b), (e) and (f) (Exhibit 11A) defining the functions of the new Department as follows:

"(b) The performance of all the functions hitherto carried out by the Information Service of the Department of Bantu Administration and Development, including the furnishing of information to the Bantu of the Republic of South Africa and the territory of South West Africa, and the supply of information concerning them and their development to the citizens of South Africa and of other countries.., . . .

"(e) The performance of all the additional services and the utilization of such media as may be effective to supply wherever it may be necessary or advisable, accurate information on all aspects of the way of life activities and natural resources of South Africa and South West Africa; and

"(f) The performance of such functions as may be decided upon from time to time."

9.241 In the meantime, after a discussion with Dr. Rhoodie, Alberts had gone into the assets of SAAN and what would be a reasonable price to pay for the shares. During August and September 1975 he reported to Dr. Rhoodie several times. He had come to the conclusion that at a price of 450 cents per share it would be a good buy and that a total amount of R9 million would be required to buy out control. It was taken for granted that the State would provide the financing. The firm of Hill Samuel had already been approached by Alberts to undertake negotiations as the broker.

9.242 It was necessary, however, to use the name of a person or body as a front to finance the take-over. This is how it came about that Mr. Louis Luyt, a well-known wealthy businessman (hereinafter referred to as "Luyt") was approached to act as such a front. According to Dr. Rhoodie this plan was put to Luyt in Dr. Rhoodie's office by him and Alberts during September 1975 and Luyt said that he was prepared to fill this role. Luyt's name was then submitted to Hill Samuel by Alberts as the person behind the takeover.

9.243 Luyt initiated negotiations almost at once. He testified that he had approached Sir De Villiers Graaff in the Cape who was prepared to put up R1-million towards a takeover of SAAN. It is not alleged that Sir De Villiers Graaff knew that Departmental funds would be used in the take-over. It is also alleged by Luyt, Alberts and Dr. Rhoodie that a certain Mr. John McGoff of the USA and a Mr. Axel Springer of Germany were approached to make money available together with the Department, Luyt and Sir De Villiers Graaff.

9.244 On October 28, 1975, however, when Alberts, according to him, was already on his way to discuss the matter with Messrs. McGoff and Springer overseas, a local Afrikaans newspaper published a report on the contemplated take over of SAAN by Luyt. This blew the whole thing, as Alberts put it. From that moment there was strong opposition from the ranks of the "English Establishment," as one witness called it, and the take-over of SAAN eventually proved impossible, even after Luyt had gone so far as to offer R12-million for control.

9.245 Early on the morning of December 4, 1975 the following men met in secret at the home of Mr. L. E. S. De Villiers in Waterkloof, Pretoria:

Dr. Mulder; Van den Bergh; Dr. Rhoodie; Dr. D. O. Rhoodie; Luyt; Du Preez, Luyt's accountant; Alberts; and Mr. L. E. S. De Villiers.

9.246 The subject for discussion was the deliberate implementation of the plan to establish an English-language newspaper themselves with moneys from the secret fund.

9.247 In this connection Dr. Rhoodie testified that he had suggested to Mr. Vorster some time previously that Luyt be used as a front for the newspaper. Although, according to Dr. Rhoodie, Mr. Vorster did not like Luyt he was persuaded that Luyt would be the best man. For that reason Luyt and his accountant, Du Preeze, would be present that morning at the meeting. After a discussion of calculations of costs drawn up by Alberts and Luyt in respect of the establishment and further financing of such a newspaper, the conclusion was reached that from R6-million to R8-million would be required. Dr. Mulder and Dr. Rhoodie undertook to make this money available from the secret funds and it was decided that Luyt should be placed in possession of the money.

9.248 Dr. Mulder's view was that the capital sum should be made available to Luyt for investment and that only the interest should be used as operating costs, and the capital, which he described as a "pool," should not be touched. That is why, Dr. Rhoodie and Alberts testified, it was decided to lend the capital to Luyt to be invested in a trust account in a bank from which the 9% or 10% interest would be paid to the company S.A. Today which would run the newspaper. Luyt and Du Preez, however, differed from these men on where it was decided the money should be invested. They contend that Luyt could invest it where he wished at the best rate of interest as long as the capital was properly secured.

9.249 The Commission does not find it necessary to determine which of these versions is the correct one since in its opinion it really makes no difference where the money was eventually invested by Luyt; the fact of the matter is that both parties are agreed that the capital was loaned to Luyt and thus became his property.

9.250 Drs. Mulder and Rhoodie in fact admit that the only condition attached to the loan was that it should be properly secured against erosion and that the interest was to be used for the operating costs of the newspaper. It is the Commission's opinion that, if a loan to a private individual from the Exchequer under the said circumstances is regarded as improper or irregular, the reprehensibility of the action already lies in the fact that the money was so taken from the Exchequer.

9.251 Seen from the angle of possible financial detriment to the State the fact that the capital eventually landed in Luyt's company [Triumph Fertilizers] is merely an aggravating fact.

9.252 The Commission will interrupt the story for a moment to point out the role played by Van den Bergh at this stage. Van den Bergh alleges that immediately after the said meeting of December 4, 1975 he reported to Mr. Vorster what had taken place and told him that Dr. Mulder and Dr. Rhoodie and Mr. L. E. S. De Villiers among others had also been there.

9.253 He contends that Mr. Vorster instructed him not to become involved in the matter, to stay away from the whole thing, but to keep his ear to the ground. Mr. Vorster contends that on the strength of what Van den Bergh had told him he had not the slightest reason to believe that the Department was involved in the establishment of the newspaper, and that he had forbidden Van den Bergh to become involved with Luyt in any way in this regard, and that he was therefore to keep away from any discussions of the matter. He furthermore said that he had told Van den Bergh that it was not Van den Bergh's function to become involved with the publication of any newspaper, either English or Afrikaans.

9.254 Mr. Vorster also alleges that Van den Bergh did not on this occasion tell him that Dr. Mulder had been present at the discussions on the establishment of the newspaper. Mr.

Vorster alleges further that, had he been informed of this, he would have spoken to Dr. Mulder and asked him not to concern himself with the matter any further.

9.255 Van den Bergh stated further that after that he did "keep his ear on the ground" and became aware almost immediately that Dr. Mulder and Dr. Rhoodie were establishing an English-language newspaper for the Department with State funds. He declares that he kept Mr. Vorster constantly informed of this and that he repeatedly told Drs. Mulder and Rhoodie that Mr. Vorster did not approve. Drs. Mulder and Rhoodie were said then to have assured him every time that Mr. Vorster was aware of their actions and approved. Every time Van den Bergh then confronted Mr. Vorster with this, Mr. Vorster was alleged to have given him the assurance that all he knew about the newspaper was what he had heard from him (Van den Bergh).

9.256 Mr. Vorster denied that he had known before 1977 that Dr. Mulder was officially involved in the newspaper. Dr. Mulder, on the other hand, testified that he was told by Van den Bergh that he had fully informed Mr. Vorster and that Mr. Vorster's reaction had been that the Bureau had nothing to do with such a newspaper but that Van den Bergh was to keep his ear to the ground and inform Mr. Vorster regularly. Dr. Mulder said that logically he interpreted this as approval of the project by Mr. Vorster. He is backed up in this by Dr. Rhoodie.

9.257 To continue the story: Luyt decided to call the newspaper the *Citizen,* and announced the establishment of "his" newspaper. Meanwhile on 29 December 1975, a total of R4 million had already been paid from secret funds in trust with Luyt's firm of auditors Malan & Du Preez. On 5 December 1975 a further R2 million was paid into the said firm of auditors from the same source, on 29 March 1976 R3.68 million and on 14 April 1976 a further amount of R320,000, bringing the total on the latter date up to R12 million.

9.258 A loan between Dr. Rhoodie and Luyt was signed on 7 April 1976 in which Dr. Rhoodie purported to lend the amount of R12 million to Luyt. The terms of that agreement were that the loan would be for a period of not less than ten years, would be interest-free for the first two years, after which interest would be payable at a rate of 3% per annum.

9.259 Since it would be patent to anyone that Dr. Rhoodie

would not have R12 million to lend, Dr. Rhoodie arranged for a letter to be sent to Luyt by a respectable Swiss financial institution on 10 August 1976 "confirming" that R12,000,000.00 had been lent to Luyt for the establishment of a newspaper, the *Citizen*.

9.260 In the meantime an amount of R220,000 had also been paid to Luyt from the secret funds on 22 January 1976 to enable the *Citizen* to sponsor the 1976 Grand Prix [automobile race].

9.261 At the meeting on 4 December 1975 it had already been discussed what policy the newspaper should follow. The proposal submitted in writing by Alberts described its envisaged character as "Independent moderate conservative, nonaligned politically."

9.262 On April 2, 1976, however, an agreement, Exhibit 3(8), was entered into between Dr. Rhoodie and Luyt containing the following provisions on this aspect:

["(d) (i) The name of the newspaper is not to be altered;

"(ii) The newspaper shall not undertake or publish anything that will endanger the social policy or economic position of the white population of the Republic of South Africa (RSA);

"(iii) The newspaper shall not in any form expound communism or promote its objectives;

"(iv) The newspaper shall not undertake or publish anything endangering the constitutionally elected government of the RSA;

"(v) The newspaper shall at all times do its best for the security of the identity and intrinsic political authority of the white population of the RSA;

"(vi) The newspaper may not be sold to any party, person, or organization by either the transfer of shares or against payment;

"(vii) Effective control of the newspaper as indicated in the terms of paragraphs (a) and (b) of this agreement is not transferable to any other individual or person or group of persons or directors of the *Citizen of S.A. Today;*

"(viii) The newspaper endorses the broad objectives of the currently elected government with respect to the separate political development of the black population and the white population of the RSA as also regarding anti-communist and security legislation of the RSA;

"(ix) All chief, sub-, assistant and contributing editors, all editors, political columnists and correspondents and editorialists of the newspaper are individually (a) bound by the editorial charter annexed hereto and signed by both parties, to sign and adhere to same, (b) to be bound to adhere to the letter and spirit of that charter and any other editorial directive that is agreed to in this contract, in the writing, editing, and publication of the *Citizen;*

"(x) No person such as described in paragraph (d) (ix) of this agreement shall be appointed to the editorial personnel of the newspaper without permission of one of the three persons named in paragraph (c)."]

9.263 From the stipulations quoted above the Commission can come to no other conclusion than that it was the intention that the newspaper should support the party policy in regard to separate development of the ruling political party. Although Dr. Mulder tried with purposeful seriousness, supported in similar fashion by Dr. Rhoodie, to convince the Commission to the contrary, the Commission was not impressed. Copies of the *Citizen* which appeared on the days immediately preceding the November 1977 election were submitted to the Commission from which it is indisputably clear that the newspaper positively encouraged voters to vote for the ruling party. (See the *Citizen* of 30 November 1977, Exhibit 12F).

9.264 It was soon apparent that the interest on the investment of R12-million was hopelessly inadequate to meet the costs of the newspaper, even at the relatively high rate of interest of $12\frac{1}{4}\%$ at which Luyt had invested the money in [Triumph Fertilizers], a company in which he held control. Luyt was not prepared, nor was he supposed to, meet the costs attached to the *Citizen* from his own pocket. He therefore soon had to turn to Dr. Rhoodie for more funds.

9.265 The acquisition of the printing press and other equipment for the proper running of the newspaper soon ran into astronomical amounts, even before the newspaper appeared on the streets. On 10 September 1976, Dr. Rhoodie was obliged to pay over a further R1 million from the secret fund for the *Citizen*, and barely three days later an additional R150,000. Without taking any interest into account, the total capital expenditure from public funds on the *Citizen* therefore amounted to R13,150 million by the end of the 1976–1977 financial year.

9.266 On 7 September 1976 the first *Citizen* appeared on the streets. During April 1977 Dr. Mulder, Dr. Rhoodie, Luyt, Du Preez and Alberts met in a room in the Holiday Inn, Jan Smuts Airport. According to their evidence, it now for the first time became clear to Drs. Mulder and Rhoodie and Alberts that Luyt had invested the R12 million in a "pool" in his company [Triumph Fertilizers], and they were bitterly dissatisfied. Hard words were spoken, there were recriminations from both sides, and at the end of a stormy session between Dr. Rhoodie and Luyt the latter told Dr. Rhoodie in strong terms what he could do with his newspaper and left the meeting with Du Preez.

9.267 After they had left the meeting, Drs. Mulder and Rhoodie and Alberts discussed the desirability of finding someone else to act as a front for the newspaper in Luyt's place, as well as possible ways of pruning the operating costs of the newspaper.

9.268 Various meetings took place subsequently at which these two aspects were discussed, and eventually Drs. Mulder and Rhoodie and Alberts, Fourie and Du Preez met in Dr. Mulder's office in Ad Astra Buildings on 29 July 1977 and had a serious discussion about the costs of the newspaper, as well as a possible take-over by someone else. It was decided to create an overdraft facility with a bank for the current losses, which at that stage proved to be in the neighbourhood of R½-million per month.

9.269 Dr. Rhoodie accordingly arranged with Volkskas, Pretoria, for an open overdraft facility for current expenses, guaranteed by the Department, and in addition for R12 million to be paid over from secret funds to the *Citizen*'s account through the front company of Thor. After the sale of Luyt's jet aircraft, in which the secret fund held a half-share through Thor, a further amount of R1,475 million of the proceeds of this half-share was paid into the *Citizen*'s account on 16 September 1977.

9.270 Up to that date, all in all, R15,825 million had been paid over as direct payments from State moneys for the account of the *Citizen*. This does not include the R220,000 provided to sponsor the 1976 Grand Prix.

9.271 Alberts had already been asked to act as financial adviser as from July 1977 and to keep an eye on the expenses of the *Citizen* by checking statements each month. Because this, it seems to the Commission, further strained relations with Luyt, a serious attempt was made to find other persons to take over the newspaper.

9.272 Mr. John McGoff, hereinafter referred to as McGoff, and Mr. Vic Jones from the U.S.A. were then invited by Dr. Rhoodie in about October 1977 to take over from Luyt.

9.273 McGoff consulted Alberts and Van Rooyen on the desirability of doing so, but both of them advised him against it. Dr. Rhoodie alleges that at that stage he discussed costs and a possible takeover of the newspaper with Mr. Vorster and that it was felt that a legal man should be brought in to keep the newspaper's affairs on an even keel. According to Dr. Rhoodie, Mr. Vorster recommended that Van Rooyen be approached to fulfil this function.

9.274 Van Rooyen was approached by Dr. Rhoodie to function as general manager of the newspaper if McGoff took over. According to Alberts, the McGoff take-over fell through, however, as a result of various factors, one being that Mr. Vorster and the S.A. Press had an agreement that no foreign company or person should gain control over a South African newspaper; McGoff, however, was in any case only interested if he could acquire more than 50 per cent of the shares in the *Citizen*. According to Dr. Rhoodie, the Department could in any case not allow control over the newspaper to pass out of its hands. Both Alberts and Van Rooyen advised McGoff to have nothing to do with the newspaper.

9.275 The newspaper had by now become a headache to all concerned. Luyt wanted to get out and was in any case no longer so welcome to Drs. Mulder and Rhoodie and Alberts.

9.276 At that critical stage Reynders appeared on the scene. After Barrie had reported to Mr. Vorster in about July 1977 that he had come upon irregular expenditure of funds in the Department, Reynders was asked by Mr. Vorster to investigate and report to him.

9.277 Reynders commenced his investigation in the course

of which he also came upon facts in connection with Project Annemarie. He was perturbed because he could not get past Van den Bergh to Mr. Vorster. The solution to this problem presented itself when he happened to meet Van Rooyen during August–September 1977 and the latter promised him that he would arrange for Reynders to see Mr. Vorster. Van Rooyen confirmed this conversation and also the fact that he then personally asked Mr. Vorster to speak to Reynders himself. Reynders testified that Mr. Vorster did in fact send for him at Libertas one evening somewhere in September 1977.

9.278 Reynders told Mr. Vorster of Van den Bergh's instructions that he was not to see Mr. Vorster without Van den Bergh's permission and he also informed Mr. Vorster of a number of irregularities he had come upon in the Department. He could not remember whether he also informed Mr. Vorster about the *Citizen* on that occasion.

9.279 Reynders is certain that he informed Mr. Vorster about the *Citizen*, but he is not quite sure of the date when he did so for the first time. He said, for example, that he had so many interviews with Mr. Vorster that it was impossible for him to say whether he had informed Mr. Vorster of the matter the first time he had seen him (496). He said that he had visited Mr. Vorster from time to time from August 1977 to April–May 1978.

9.280 According to Reynders, he had, however, kept Mr. Vorster regularly informed of how the expenditure from the Exchequer was mounting month by month, that at one stage it had exceeded R18 million, and that in addition there was an overdrawn account at Volkskas from which the *Citizen* supplemented its deficits monthly. He also testified that Mr. Vorster regularly questioned him about the state of the newspaper's finances.

9.281 During November 1977, before the general election, a meeting was convened at the home of Mr. Vorster at Libertas, Pretoria, where the following were present that evening: Mr. Vorster, Reynders, Dr. Mulder, Dr. Rhoodie, Van den Bergh and Alberts. According to Reynders, the meeting had been called so that Mr. Vorster could confront those concerned with the detailed information with which Reynders had already furnished Mr. Vorster. According to Van Rooyen, he had also already at that stage informed Mr. Vorster of the fact that the Department was financing a daily newspaper.

9.282 At the meeting Reynders proceeded to give a detailed explanation, with reference to written notes, of a number of projects, including Project Annemarie, in which after investigation he was prima facie of the opinion that irregularities could have been committed.

9.283 Although those notes (Exhibit 7D) bear the date 30 November 1977, Reynders maintains that that meeting took place before that date.

9.284 According to Reynders all these facts had a very depressing effect on Mr. Vorster, so much so that he was taken ill at about 11:30 that evening and excused himself. Drs. Mulder and Rhoodie tried to justify their actions to Mr. Vorster that evening according to Reynders. No conclusion was, however, reached because Mr. Vorster became ill (508).

9.285 Mr. Vorster confirmed that the meeting had taken place and that Reynders had informed him on that occasion that over R20 million had already been spent on the *Citizen*. He testified further that Dr. Mulder then assured him that the money was safe, and that on that and various other occasions he had debated the principle with Dr. Mulder of utilising public funds for an undertaking of that kind. He had put it clear to Dr. Mulder that it was not morally or ethically justifiable.

9.286 Dr. Mulder held the opposite view and pointed out to Mr. Vorster that the fact that there was no objective English-language newspaper in South Africa constituted a lack.

9.287 Mr. Vorster also made it clear that Mr. Mulder had continued to run the newspaper against his (Mr. Vorster's) wishes, but that he (Mr. Vorster) could do nothing about it because he regarded it as spilt milk.

The following excerpt from the record is quoted verbatim by the Commission:

[*Question:* "Yes, but milk was still constantly spilt every day after that."

Reply (Mr. Vorster): "Exactly, because it was necessary to compute the government's liability, and in view of the contractual obligations the government had landed into as a consequence of that situation . . ." (794) "A calculation was made, which I understand—I am speaking now wholly by report—about what happened after I lost touch with this matter. Whether it is now advantageous for the government to terminate it right away or whether it would be more profitable for the government to put an end to it later on."]

9.288 This was November 1977. When Mr. Vorster retired as Prime Minister on 28 September 1978 the *Citizen* was still fully controlled by the State and the State was still subsidising a monthly loss of up to about R400 000.

9.289 Dr. Mulder's and Dr. Rhoodie's consensus of opinion at the beginning of 1978 was that the newspaper should be taken away from Luyt. That is why Alberts and one Mr. Jussen were approached to take over the newspaper and run it as a front for the Department. At first they were reluctant to do so, but later agreed and decided to do it "for their country's good." So far as the outside world was concerned, a consortium, consisting of Alberts and Jussen, took over the *Citizen* in February 1978. The Department undertook to supply the newspaper with funds from the Exchequer for at least two years, after which Alberts and Jussen would try to run it for their own profit if they could get it on to a profitable basis.

9.290 When Alberts and Jussen took over the *Citizen* it was still costing the State the following:

1) Total of direct payments referred to above — R15,825,000
2) Total of overdrawn account with Volkskas utilised for the benefit of *The Citizen* — R 7,468,031
3) Payment to sponsor Grand Prix 1976 — R 220,000
4) Guarantee to Volkskas for M.G.D. Graphic Systems for rotary press equipment — 77,594,770
5) Interest received from [Triumph Fertilizer] for investment of R12 million — R 2 684 461

Total — R26,792,262

9.291 This was still not the end of it. On 14 February 1978 an amount of R339, 857-21 was paid into Alberts's account with Volkskas through a Swiss bank for the account of the *Citizen* from the proceeds of the sale of shares held by the Department.

9.292 On 17 February 1978 and 14 March the balance of the proceeds from the sale of the shares was transferred to Alberts's account with Volkskas through a Swiss bank for the account of the *Citizen* in two instalments of R897,605–78 and R2 179,408–90, respectively.

9.293 On 14 June 1978 a further amount of R443,470–73 was transferred from a secret account of the Department in Switzerland for the account of the newspaper.

9.294 During August 1978 Van Den Bergh authorised the payment of R50,000 from funds of the Department already in Alberts's possession for another project for the account for the *Citizen*.

9.295 During August 1978 a guarantee was given to Volkskas Industriele Bank by means of an investment from secret funds for the printing costs of the *Citizen* to the amount of R450,000. The Commission regards this as expenditure on behalf of the *Citizen*.

9.296 After August 1978 a further amount of R705,000 was used by Alberts from secret funds in other projects on behalf of the *Citizen*.

9.297 The total amount utilised from public funds during the period of Alberts's management up to the date of appointment of the Commission therefore amounted to R5,115,470–73.

9.298 All in all, from the date of establishment of the *Citizen* up to the date of the Commission's appointment, the *Citizen* cost the State R26,792,262 during the Luyt period and R5,115,470–73 according to paragraph 9.297 above, i.e. R31,907,732–73.

9.299 To recover the initial investment of R12 million from [Triumph] after Luyt had left the *Citizen* an agreement between Dr. Rhoodie and Luyt was signed on 8 June 1978 under which the amount of R13,983,022 would be repaid by Luyt over a period of seven years into a bank account stipulated by Rhoodie.

The instalments were to be paid as follows:

Appendix A

2 March 1979	R 505,904
2 March 1980	R 505,904
2 March 1981	R1,005,904
2 March 1982	R2,644,446
2 March 1983	R2,494,446
2 March 1984	R2,344,446
2 March 1985	R2,194,446
2 March 1986	R2,287,526
	R13,983,022

(Exhibit 3)

9.300 The total of R13,983,022 consists of a capital sum of R10,118,080–00, plus interest on this sum for the period.

9.301 The difference between the R12 million and the R10,118,080–00 appears to be due to a loss of interest suffered by Luyt because Standard Bank had raised their rate of interest on a foreign loan to Luyt from 3% to 12% when Luyt's involvement with the *Citizen* became known to them. Because the Department had given the undertaking that Luyt would not suffer any loss from his own pocket as a result of his connection with the *Citizen* he was compensated for the loss by its deduction from the R12 million debt.

(Author's note: That concluded the *Citizen* story as far as the Erasmus commission's initial findings went. Moreover, in the next chapter of the December 1978 report, the commission said (par. 10.337) that it "must be stated clearly and unequivocally that Mr. Vorster's attitude and actions throughout all the activities involving irregularities were, in the Commission's opinion, honest, bona fide and devoid of any trace of personal gain. In the Commission's opinion his integrity is unblemished." But by the time the body handed in its final report on 30 May 1979, a much different picture had emerged.)

3.1 At the time when the report was prepared the Commission had no absolute certainty as to when Mr. Vorster first became aware of the State financing of the *Citizen*. All the witnesses who gave evidence on this matter (except Drs. Mulder and Rhoodie, who were found to be unreliable in this connection), such as Reynders, Advocate Van Rooyen and Mr. Vorster himself, agreed that it was during the latter half of 1977, but could not pinpoint a specific time. They did, however, all agree that he had been informed of several apparent cases of misappropriation by the Department, including the *Citizen*, at the latest during November 1977 at the evening meeting at his residence, Libertas.

3.2 For this reason the Commission gave Mr. Vorster the benefit of the doubt in its report, and found that he became aware of the implications of the *Citizen* only at the end of November. The Commission was naturally mindful of the fact that much earlier knowledge could have serious implications for Mr. Vorster, and in all fairness it was not prepared to make a speculative finding on such an important aspect.

3.3 Mr. Vorster himself was unsure about the date when he had heard. He gave evidence to this effect at pp. V. 792 and 793: ["Now, can I put it to you this way, that the *Citizen* project was made known to you and that government funds were involved in the matter around August to September 1977? I do not want to limit myself to a definite date, it could have been any time from when Mr. Barrie spoke of it to MW until right now. I cannot tell you just when." (V 1939)]

3.4 Reynders was also uncertain about when he had informed Mr. Vorster of the irregularities relating to the *Citizen* and could be sure only of November 1977 as a date when Mr. Vorster was fully informed (V 9.279).

3.5 Advocate Van Rooyen was also fairly vague, to the extent that he did not fix the time closer than ["during the second half of 1977"] (V 47 and V 50).

3.6 This uncertainty has, however, now been cleared up for the Commission by Mr. Vorster himself in a press statement released on 22 March 1979, which was submitted to the Commission. In this statement Mr. Vorster makes it clear that he became aware of the matter as early as August 1977.

3.7 Referring to the *Citizen*, Mr. Vorster says in his statement:

["I asked him (Dr. Mulder) why he had never discussed this business (the *Citizen*) personally with me. He had not only seen me every Tuesday at the cabinet meetings, but he had seen me on various other occasions and why had he not told me of the matter? Why had he not informed me and why was the first news I had of it to come from Mr. Barrie in that connection in August 1977? His answer was that he had not wanted to compromise me by speaking to me about the matter."] (1925–1926)

3.8 On being questioned by the Commission on 27 April 1979, Mr. Vorster also testified that he had been informed of the State's involvement in the *Citizen* by Reynders during September 1977.

3.9 For purposes of the Commission's interim report, several ministers who had served in Mr. Vorster's Cabinet gave evidence during March 1979 that it was not until his last Cabinet meeting on 26 September 1978 that Mr. Vorster informed the Cabinet about the *Citizen* for the first time, and then only after he had been confronted by some members of the Cabinet the previous evening with the facts that Van Rooyen had given them.

3.10 The Commission can find no fault with the fact that, when the facts about the *Citizen* came to his knowledge, Van Rooyen confidentially informed Mr. Vorster of them. It was after all no more than his duty as a citizen to inform the country's highest figure of authority confidentially and out of loyalty about what he regarded as a serious irregularity in the spending of the taxpayer's money.

3.11 However, the Commission finds Mr. Vorster's reaction to this step taken by Van Rooyen strange. The Commission quotes Mr. Vorster's evidence on this point:

[". . . Will you allow me, Mr. Commissioner, to say a word. Because I was dragged in by Van Rooyen's evidence, to say a few words about Van Rooyen . . . I have known Van Rooyen for quite a number of years . . .

"Very garrulous, and you, during your practice as an attorney, must have known how such juniors speak with other people about how they lead their seniors. And he gladly played the senior when he was talking to you; he's a smooth talker and an interesting gossiper. He told me in the course of time what he was in Southwest Africa; now and then he asked if he could come and see me, what they were considering in the gymnasium discussions and how things were tending in the Southwest. I found that very interesting and listened to him willingly. In other words, he had free access to my home. When this Barrie investigation came up, he (Attorney Van Rooyen) visited me on a few occasions. He brought me amusement. But the facts he put before me were at that stage already known to me and everybody; I had heard it either at Barrie's or at Reynders's. There was nothing useful in what he told me, but he had a lot of nice gossip from Rhoodie, with whom he was friendly . . ." (V 755 to V 767).]

3.12 From this reaction of Mr. Vorster's it now seems to the Commission, in the new light of the March 1979 evidence, as if he feels resentment towards Van Rooyen, blames him and regards him as a gossip-monger for ever having told him (Mr. Vorster) the facts and for having revealed them to members of his Cabinet in September 1978.

3.13 The Commission can find no fault with Van Rooyen's action in revealing the facts about the *Citizen* to members of the Cabinet on the eve of the election of a new Prime Minister in 1978, especially if it is remembered that he knew that Dr. Mulder, one of the candidates, had had a hand in this gross irregularity.

3.14 Evidence given by Mr. Vorster before December 1978 about the irregularities consisted mainly of denials, and the Commission accepted his denials rather than the evidence of witnesses such as General Van den Bergh, Dr. Mulder and Dr. Rhoodie that contradicted the denials. The Commission did not want to make findings against him on uncertain evidence.

3.15 One piece of evidence given by General Van den Bergh, however, impressed the Commission as being the truth because it was given spontaneously and as coming from an old friend of Mr. Vorster's, who was moved by the recollection of a painful moment. The Commission finds Mr. Vorster's reaction to this strange and unacceptable.

3.16 The evidence deals with General Van den Bergh's visit to Cape Town to say goodbye to Mr. Vorster. While he was in the aircraft, General Van den Bergh stated, he sat there turning over in his mind what he had to go and say to Mr. Vorster in Cape Town.

Appendix A

3.17 His evidence reads as follows:

["And then my thoughts turned to this terrible problem with which the poor man was struggling, the *Citizen*, for I knew it had become a twinge of conscience for him. How can I help him? I made several attempts to help him . . . I came to the Cape and visited him immediately. I made the report on my business and then said to him, 'John, I want to speak to you very seriously today man to man, friend to friend. Just you and I. We've come a long way. You know, John, how much I admire you, how much I esteem you . . . but you've now reached a stage where things are not going well. It's not good, and it pains me. I don't want people criticizing you. As to me, they can say what they like, but they must leave you alone. Here in this lobby, I hear people blaming you among themselves in connection with this information business. They say you're not telling the truth. They don't say you're lying in what you say, but they do say you have knowledge which you're holding back. And it is true they say (that) you're not telling the truth. I know, John, and best of everything is, you know that is so. And you know that I know that is so. And you know Connie Mulder knows it's so.' He shrugged his shoulders, then he said, 'Yes, that's so.' Then I said, 'But John, that can't go on. You must dispose of this matter; it's eating into you like a cancer; we can't go on like this. And your health is not good.' " (V 942).]

3.18 When this evidence was read to Mr. Vorster, he replied:

["That's too silly for words. Such a conversation never took place. That is presumptuous as anything I've ever heard." (V 1960).]

That General Van den Bergh is indeed presumptuous, is clear from Appendix A, attached, but the Commission is of the opinion that the version of the incident he gave here was free of fabrication or pretence.

3.19 On the grounds of Mr. Vorster's own evidence given on 27 April 1979, as well as the statement contained in his press release, the Commission therefore finds that he knew of the *Citizen* project as early as August or September 1977, and this admission by him has given certainty about evidence about which there was no certainty before December 1978.

B. *The Implication of This Finding*

(a) Mr. Vorster's evidence therefore does not tell the correct story.

(i) Mr. Vorster and General Van den Bergh.

3.20 At all material times Mr. Vorster was the Prime Minister of the Republic of South Africa, and in that capacity he was in a position where one would normally expect him to know how the Department obtained its finances and also to know about its most important projects.

3.21 In fact, Mr. Vorster referred to these matters in his letter to the Ministers of Finance, Defence, etc., in December 1973. This letter is quoted in V 9.239. In it he said that the growing political and propaganda onslaught on the RSA was making new demands on the Department and that, among other things, the means available to the Department had to be adapted to the situation and that the Minister of Information should consult the Prime Minister on important projects.

3.22 The Bureau for State Security was established under Mr. Vorster in his Department. General Van den Bergh was placed in charge and he was in control of a secret fund in the Bureau for State Security. The first secret funds for the Department's secret funds were channelled from the Department of Defence through the Bureau for State Security. The position is explained in paragraphs V 2.12 to V 2.17.

3.23 Specific reference is made there to the letter from the Secretary to the Treasury to the Secretary for State Security, dated 29 March 1973, in which it was stated that Mr. Vorster had been and was being consulted in this connection.

3.24 One would find it perfectly natural and logical that General Van den Bergh, as informant, would know of these arrangements, regarding not only the Department's money but also its major projects because of their highly secret and sensitive nature.

3.25 Concerning General Van den Bergh's connection with the Department, Mr. Vorster gave the following evidence:

["Do you know if there were any reasons why General Van den Bergh should have been disquieted regarding the activities of the department?—There was no official reason that I know of to be worried in that connection, besides the bureau kept an eye on practically everything, did it not? That was the nature of their function to look into every hole and corner to see if there was anything to concern them or not. But there were no instructions or official reasons why he would have to be concerned." V 804.]

(ii) Mr. Vorster's knowledge of the financial arrangements.

3.26 At pages V 803 and V 804 of Mr. Vorster's evidence, the minutes of the Commission read as follows:

["Mr. President (Prime Minister), did you know that money from the defense secret funds had passed through the bureau to the information department? Oddly enough . . . I learned only comparatively recently that it had been channeled that way."]

3.27 He intimated that he had become aware of this only about 8 May (1978). After he had replied to the first question in the negative, the Commissioner concerned said:

["My next question ought to (have) been whether you were responsible for that arrangement.—No, I was not responsible for that arrangement nor was I cognizant of it. I discovered this year for the first time that that was the practice." (V 803).]

3.28 Senator Owen Horwood's evidence (V 1933) paints a completely different picture. He said that on 21 February 1975, shortly after he had become Minister of Finance, Dr. Diederichs had told him that this arrangement had been agreed upon by Mr. Vorster, himself and Dr. Mulder (V 1934). Senator Horwood's evidence continues as follows:

". . . and I would like to add to that, Mr. Chairman, that I did some time later, talk to the Prime Minister (Mr. Vorster) about this. He said it is correct that there was this decision which was felt to be in the national interest, very strongly, and it was felt that this was the best way to do it. In other words he did confirm what Dr. Diederichs had told me.

"And this was continued in spite of the objection of Mr. Botha, . . . ?—Correct."

3.29 General Van den Bergh supports Senator Horwood's evidence. It appears from this that Mr. Vorster was aware of all the basic financial arrangements right from the start, and that Mr. P. W. Botha objected to them from the start, a fact that was denied by Mr. Vorster (V 804).

3.30 Among other things General Van den Bergh said (V 829 et sequor) that Mr. Vorster had instructed Dr. Rhoodie to check the Department's books and that Mr. Vorster had also said that Mr. P. W. Botha had objected to the arrangement, but that despite this objection this had to be done. Right at the start there were objections to the arrangement (V 830 and V 905). [Also see TV 60 and TV 61 and the evidence of Mr. Pretorius (1615).]

3.31 It is reasonable to infer from the above that Mr. Vorster must in fact have known everything about the basic financial arrangements in connection with the Department's funds (see V 10.316) and its main projects, and this finding, on the probabilities and the direct evidence quoted above, is borne out by the correspondence. In this connection, Dr. Rhoodie's letter, dated 4 February 1977, to the Secretary to the Treasury (Exhibit 17E 6) may be referred to as an additional factor. The second paragraph reads:

["My minister informed me today that he is not prepared to disclose details on Senekal project (this included the *Citizen* project). He makes a complete annual report to the Prime Minister."]

3.32 The Commission refers further to paragraphs TV 52 and TV 53, in which the procedure followed by Dr. Rhoodie, the Minister of the Department and Mr. Vorster is described. Only after this procedure was the Minister of Finance approached for the money. [Exhibits 17D, 17E 1 (dated 13 December 1976), 17E 3 (dated 21 January 1977), 17E 4 (dated 24 January 1977) and 17E 5 (dated 2 February 1977).]

(iii) Mr. Vorster's knowledge of the secret projects.

3.33 From all these letters it is furthermore clear that Mr. Vorster was consulted in advance concerning the funds needed for the secret projects. It therefore seems highly unlikely that the secret projects would not have been mentioned to him to support the requests in terms of Mr. Vorster's letter of December 1973, which is referred to in paragraph 3.40 and the concluding paragraph of which reads as follows:

["The Minister of Information fully discussed the nature of the matter with the Prime Minister concerning these important information aspects and plans."]

Appendix A

3.34 More particularly as regards the *Citizen*, in the light of the above finding and information there are indications that General Van den Bergh would have informed Mr. Vorster about the progress of the newspaper, as he testified and did on Mr. Vorster's instructions to keep his ear to the ground. The Commission will not, however, make any specific finding about the knowledge that Mr. Vorster had of the *Citizen* before August 1977.

(b) Mr. Vorster kept the irregularities secret.

3.35 So far as keeping irregularities secret is concerned, the Commission does not intend to deal with the whole sequence of events since 1973, but wants to single out only a few incidents.

(i) The Certificate issued by Reynders.

3.36 As a result of the evidence given on this matter by several Ministers after December 1978 (1940 to 1946 and 1970), the Commission has some comments supplementary to the report on Mr. Vorster's action concerning Reynders's report to him dated 19 September 1978.

3.37 The Commission has already dealt with the certificate in the report (see V 11.376 to V 11.387) with reference to the actions of Dr. Mulder and General Van den Bergh and the pressure they exerted on Reynders to submit a false certificate to Mr. Vorster.

3.38 The Commission found that Mr. Vorster had not known in what circumstances the report had come to him nor that it was a false report submitted to him. When questioned in April 1979, however, Mr. Vorster took the line that he had been satisfied with the report and that it had not been false, even after the nature of the irregularities then existing had been pointed out to him. The Commission finds this unacceptable. In the light of this the Commission has to reconsider its original view on Mr. Vorster's involvement in the false version of the real situation in that report.

3.39 In his most recent evidence General Van den Bergh maintained that Reynders had to investigate any irregularities, whatever their nature. This was also the opinion of several members of the Cabinet (see 1940 and 1946). The report came before the Cabinet on 26 September 1978. Mr. A. Schlebusch, Minister of the Interior, gave evidence that he had had the impression that Mr. Vorster was not happy with the report at that time. Mr. Schlebusch himself had not been happy with the report, and said that he would not have accepted it (1955 and 1957).

3.40 Mr. Vorster tried to defend the certificate and would have accepted it as being quite in order and in accordance with his instructions to Reynders. According to him it had not been necessary for Dr. Mulder or General Van den Bergh to exert any pressure on Reynders (V 792).

3.41 Mr. Vorster said in evidence that many stories had been doing the rounds and that, when he had instructed Reynders to investigate the alleged irregularities he had had in mind only cases of ["self-enrichment and financial embezzlement."] (V 791).

3.42 Reynders was adamant that he would not have issued such a certificate had it not been for the pressure exerted on him. He therefore probably understood the instruction as being different from what Mr. Vorster now says the intention was. He also gave evidence that he had reported Dr. Mulder's conversation with him to Mr. Vorster, and that Mr. Vorster had then forbidden him to make such a report (V 11.380).

3.43 The Commission finds it difficult to understand why Mr. Vorster did not give Reynders the instruction concerning the investigation that he says was his intention. Mr. Vorster has issued a press statement, Exhibit 10D, stating exactly what his instruction to Reynders was, viz "To make a complete and thorough investigation of all asserted irregularities, accusations, stories and rumors so far as they relate to the abuse of funds." In this sense, surely, the massive spending of State funds on the *Citizen* and the loan of R825000 by Dr. Rhoodie to Pieterse for the making of a film for his personal gain, for example, would have been serious irregularities committed in the Department.

3.44 When Mr. Vorster received Reynders's report, he had already been informed in detail by Reynders over the preceding period of almost a year of a large number of irregularities, including the two cases of gross misappropriation of State funds mentioned above. Despite this, Reynders then reported in writing to Mr. Vorster that his investigation had revealed no cases of misappropriation.

Appendix A

3.45 The Commission believes that to Mr. Vorster's knowledge on the date of Reynders report Reynders had deliberately painted an incorrect picture of the ture state of affairs, and that there were in fact cases of gross misappropriation in the Department.

3.46 Mr. Vorster explained this untenable situation to the Commission by saying that at the time when he received the report he had been concerned only about whether "somebody had been filling his own pockets" and whether there had been self-enrichment and embezzlement. He gave this as the reason why he had accepted Reynders's report without a murmur (V 783–792).

3.47 The Commission cannot accept this explanation of Mr. Vorster's. He knew at that stage that serious misappropriations, in terms of his own instruction to Reynders, had taken place in the Department and he therefore knew that Reynders's report was concealing those irregularities. By accepting it and publishing it to the Cabinet, still without revealing his knowledge of all the true facts to the Cabinet, he was not only doing the members of his Cabinet an injustice but was in fact participating in action which in itself was a serious irregularity, viz the covering up of gross irregularities. To this extent Mr. Vorster must share the responsibility with Dr. Mulder for the latter's irregular actions.

3.48 On 27 April 1979, however, Mr. Vorster gave evidence that when he first confronted Dr. Mulder about the *Citizen*, he put it to him unequivocally that it was ["wrongful allocation"] of State Funds. The Commission can see no difference between ["wrongful allocation"] and ["misappropriation"] of State funds.

3.49 Despite the view he expressed outspokenly to Dr Mulder he accepted Reynders's statement in his report that there was "misappropriation" of State funds by the Department.

3.50 Mr. Vorster wanted to explain this obvious contradiction by intimating that such wrong spending was not necessarily morally wrong. In the Commission's judgment, however, Mr. Vorster has only two alternatives: either the spending on the *Citizen* was wrong and therefore, as a misappropriation morally unacceptable to him, or it was morally acceptable to him and therefore no misappropriation. If the latter alternative is his view, that may explain among other things, why for more than year he took no steps to stop the State spending on the *Citizen*.

3.51 Apart from the fact that Mr. Vorster himself was also, inter alia, responsible for the arrangement to channel the secret funds to the Department and did not stop certain projects as soon as possible after they had come to his knowledge, the Commission also holds Mr. Vorster to blame for concealing his knowledge of the irregularities.

(ii) Dr. Mulder's denial in Parliament.

3.52 In his evidence before the Commission in November 1978 Mr. Vorster denied that he had given a note to Dr. Mulder during the Parliamentary Session in 1978 telling him to say in reply to a question put by by Mr. J. D. du P. Basson [see Hansard (1978), Columns 6499 to 6500] that the government ["does not own a newspaper and does not run one either."]

3.53 Dr. Mulder contended that Mr. Vorster had in fact given him such a note when he had asked Mr. Vorster's advice on how to reply to the question. In December the Commission was not prepared to give a decision on this evidence since Dr. Mulder's statement was unsupported against Mr. Vorster's denial, and the Commission was in any case not much impressed by Dr. Mulder's efforts in general to excuse himself.

3.54 In April 1979, however, Mr. I. W. van den Heever, who had been Dr. Mulder's private secretary at the time, appeared before the Commission and gave evidence that he had seen a note to this effect in Mr. Vorster's handwriting among Dr. Mulder's documents after the debate.

3.55 Mr. Vorster had denied that he wrote the note in dispute at Dr. Mulder's request, and intimated that, on another occasion and on some subject other than the *Citizen*, he had given a written reply to Dr. Mulder. Mr. Vorster has denied that he was present in the House of Asembly when Dr. Mulder replied to the question concerned. In the circumstances the Commission is in doubt as to what the truth is, and is again not prepared to make a specific finding on this matter.

(c) Mr. Vorster conceals the irregularities from the Cabinet, regardless of the consequences.

3.56 If it is now accepted as beyond all doubt that Mr.

Vorster was informed of the facts about the *Citizen* as early as August or September 1977, this means that he kept the facts from the Cabinet for more than a year. The fact that, in the Commission's judgment, he was virtually compelled by Advocate Van Rooyen's actions to inform the Cabinet at the eleventh hour, before he retired as Prime Minister, casts shadow over Mr. Vorster's committedness at the time to open administration of the country and the sharing of responsibility. The Cabinet is, after all, the highest executive authority, and has a right, because of the tremendous burden of its collective responsibility, to know all the facts that might have a bearing on that responsibility.

3.57 The Commission has reason to believe that, had it not been for Advocate Van Rooyen and the subsequent firm action taken by Ministers P. W. Botha, R. F. Botha, Schlebusch and Heunis, the serious irregularities that took place in the Department while Mr. Vorster was Prime Minister would have remained hidden from the next Prime Minister, and he would have had to find out about them himself. If Dr. Mulder had, perhaps precisely by reason of such concealment, become the new Prime Minister, the concealment could, in our opinion, logically have been continued to protect Dr. Mulder, who had after all fathered the *Citizen*.

3.58 If the irregularities had remained concealed from Mr. P. W. Botha until after he had become the Prime Minister, he could have found himself plunged without warning into a storm, the consequences of which could hardly have been foreseen.

3.59 Since the Commission issued its report, Dr. Mulder has been obliged to resign from his office as a Member of Parliament because of the irregularities in which he was involved. In his statement to the press on 22 March 1979 Mr. Vorster reproached Dr. Mulder for remaining silent when his colleagues in the Cabinet were accused by the Parliamentary opposition and certain newspapers of being implicated in these irregularities.

3.60 In essence, however, a similar reproach can be addressed to Mr. Vorster in the Commission's judgment. For more than a year Mr. Vorster together with Dr. Mulder, kept his knowledge of irregularities in the administration of the country from his Cabinet colleagues, at a time when the press and the opposition were already making serious insinuations and accusations of maladministration against the Government. During this period every innocent member of the Cabinet therefore had, because of the collective responsibility of the Cabinet, to bear the stigma of public accusations without knowing all the facts. The Commission does, however, in all fairness to Mr. Vorster, want to point out again that he did have the affairs of the Department investigated, for example by the Public Service Commission and others during this period.

3.61 In the Commission's judgment nobody can be reproached for mere knowledge, per se, of irregularities, unless such a person is in a position where it could reasonably be expected of him to take positive steps to rectify matters. If it is accepted that Mr. Vorster became aware of the *Citizen* (and other irregularities) as early as August–September 1977, and that he as Prime Minister was in a position where he could have intervened drastically to put a stop to the mischief, his earlier knowledge from August to November 1977 places a different complexion on his actions.

3.62 In passing, the Commission would point out that, as early as December 1975, General Van den Bergh informed Mr. Vorster about the presence of executive officers of the Department at the foundation meeting of a newspaper at the home of De Villiers on 4 December 1975 (see V 9.253 to V 9.255). Although Mr. Vorster contends that he was not given the impression by General Van den Bergh that the Department was involved in the establishment of the newspaper, it seems strange to the Commission that he did not have a closer investigation undertaken after he had heard that his head of security had been present and the Department well represented at the foundation meeting.

3.63 The Commission finds it significant that he instructed General Van den Bergh not to involve himself with the newspaper. Whatever other conclusions may be drawn from this, one thing is clear: Mr. Vorster unequivocally showed his disapproval of State involvement in the newspaper.

3.64 For this reason it must have come as a shock to Mr. Vorster when, in August or September 1977, he found out that the Department was involved. One would reasonably have expected that Mr. Vorster would then immediately have called in Dr. Mulder or Dr. Rhoodie or both and would have compelled them to stop the State financing of the *Citizen* without delay.

3.65 In fact Mr. Vorster did nothing of the kind, and, according to his own evidence, merely discussed the propriety of financing the *Citizen* with Dr. Mulder. He was also shocked. He did not, however, take any firm action to rectify matters. On the contrary, he called an election in the full knowledge of all the irregularities, without sharing the facts either with his Cabinet or with his caucus and without calling Dr. Mulder to account. It seems to the Commission that he began looking for a solution only after the election. Even then he did nothing effective to sever the State's connections with the newspaper, except to ["discuss"] the morality of the matter repeatedly with Dr. Mulder.

3.66 The Commission finds this behaviour on the part of Mr. Vorster from August 1977 onwards unacceptable despite his state of health, for somebody in his position with the views that, according to what he says himself, he held about State financing of a newspaper.

(d) Why did he not reveal the facts?

3.67 The Commission does not want to speculate about this but would like to quote a passage from Advocate Van Rooyen's evidence. The evidence reads:

["At one stage I asked him (Mr. Vorster) if there was not an element of blackmail in the case, because I had heard what I had discussed with him, that Dr. Eschel Rhoodie is threatening to bring the government down if any action was brought against him. That was now hearsay, but I had discussed it with the Prime Minister at that time, and then I asked the Prime Minister if there was not an element of blackmail in that connection and in the whole affair, to which the Prime Minister answered me 'one thousand percent. He holds my ministers' political life in the palm of his hand.' That was alarming to me."]

3.68 Even this piece of evidence given by Advocate Van Rooyen later proved to be true.

C. *Conclusions and Finding*

(a) Conclusions.

3.69 On the basis of its findings in this chapter the Commission has come to the following conclusions and finding:

(i) Mr. Vorster knew everything about the basic financial arrangements for the Department's fund (3.31).

(ii) He was consulted about the secret funds as well as the projects themselves (3.33).

(iii) Because he did not reveal irregularities that came to his attention (3.35); concealed them from the Cabinet (3.54) and delayed, for this considerable period, taking purposeful steps to put an end to this wrong state of affairs he is jointly responsible for the fact that the irregularities continued, including the *Citizen*.

(b) Finding.

3.70 The Commission's finding in the last paragraph of par. V 10.377 stands amended in the light of the findings and conclusions in this chapter.

Appendix B:
John McGoff and the *Washington Star*

THE STAR PROJECT,
DR. MULDER AND THE OUTCOME

A. *The* Star *Project*
   (a) Mr. John McGoff.
   10.1 Mr. John McGoff, hereinafter referred to as McGoff, a publisher of about 40 medium-sized newspapers in Michigan and a friend of several American politicians, visited South Africa in 1968 at the suggestion of De Villiers. De Villiers described him to the Commission as an Irish American who feels intensely and strongly about the things he believes in. And one of the things in which he believed, according to De Villiers, was that the RSA had a role to play together with the USA, and that as a Western power South Africa should be preserved for the USA. It was these views that prompted McGoff to come to South Africa in 1968 on invitation (150).

   10.2 It was said that during this visit he discovered an affinity with South Africa and her people, which he cultivated further. After that he was regularly in touch with the RSA and did things for South Africa without being paid for them. For instance, when De Villiers requested him to get a message across to the Americans in an article about the Republic, he would simply send the article through to all his editors and say: "Look, this article has to be published" and it would be done.

   10.3 In May 1971 Dr. Mulder and Barrie visited the USA (see Barrie's evidence).

   McGoff was said to have arranged numerous interviews

and meetings with important Americans for them without receiving any remuneration. According to De Villiers, McGoff was on very friendly terms with the Jordanian Royal Family and with Israel. He knew President Nixon well and was a personal friend of the then Vice-President Ford, to whom he introduced Dr. Mulder in the USA. On occasion, according to the witness, he was invited to the White House by President Carter. He was also a keen supporter of the Republican Party in the USA.

10.4 De Villiers testified that the Arabs had offered McGoff a certain sum of money to buy them a newspaper in the USA. He did not accept it, however, because he did not share their ideologies and would not be able to work with them. According to the witness, McGoff, as a newspaperman, had the gift of turning a newspaper in financial straits into a profitable proposition.

(b) The RSA decides to buy the *Washington Star* and shares.

10.5 This is how it came about that in 1974 McGoff indicated that the *Washington Star* was in financial difficulties, and that it could be bought. With his acumen he would be able to turn the newspaper into a more profitable enterprise.

10.6 For understandable reasons such a newspaper, in the heart of Washington could, according to De Villiers, do a great deal for South Africa if it had a positive attitude towards the Republic.

10.7 According to the witness, the influence of the *Washington Star* was not confined to Washington, but extended countrywide. In Washington itself there is another big newspaper, viz the *Washington Post,* which is very unsympathetic towards the RSA. The *New York Times,* which is also in circulation in Washington is, according to him, also basically anti-South Africa.

10.8 After the approach by McGoff, the *Star* project began. De Villiers informed Dr. Rhoodie of the circumstances. Dr. Rhoodie is said then to have discussed the matter with Dr. Mulder. The witness was told that Dr. Mulder, in his turn, had discussed it with Mr. Vorster (then the Prime Minister) and Dr. Diederichs (115).

10.9 Mr. Gerald Browne, the then Secretary for Finance, hereinafter referred to as Browne, also testified that Dr.

Diederichs had told him that the project had been initiated by Mr. Vorster and Dr. Mulder (1297 and 1301).

10.10 On 27 April 1979 Mr. Vorster testified that he was aware of the transfer of $10,000,000 but that he had had nothing to do with it. He stated that Drs. Diederichs and Mulder had discussed the matter with him at the time and that he had then told them that he was completely against it. They had asked him not to stand in the way of their buying the newspaper and he had promised not to do so, but he had said that they were not to involve (["trouble"]) him. He later learned that the purchase of the *Washington Star* had fallen through.

10.11 The idea of buying the newspaper met with the approval of the Department, and it was initially decided to negotiate with the Union Bank of Switzerland with a view to getting the bank to make a loan to the RSA for that purpose. The late Dr. Diederichs first discussed the possibility of such a loan with the bank in Zurich and later sent De Villiers, Browne and Dr. D. O. Rhoodie to Zurich to follow up the matter of a loan (115 and 1298).

10.12 The reason why a loan was considered in the first place, was that McGoff told De Villiers he needed about $25,000,000 for the transaction. He himself could put up about $15,000,000 and asked that the RSA should contribute the other $10,000,000.

(c) Transfer of $10,000,000.

10.13 In the RSA it was decided that the $10,000,000 for the purchase of the *Washington Star* would provisionally come out of the Special Defence Account of the Department of Defence. The project was regarded as top secret, and so large a sum of money could not be provided from the Department's Vote without revealing the existence of the project. Browne was accordingly instructed by the Minister of Finance to make the transfer through the Department of Defence. The amount was transferred to the above-mentioned bank in Zurich at the end of September 1974 (see TV 57 *et sequor*) and from there it was invested in McGoff's account in the USA.

10.14 According to Browne's evidence it was soon clear from their talks in Zurich with Dr. Saager of the bank, McGoff and his adviser, a Mr. Jones, that the matter of a loan need not be discussed any further. The important point, however, was how the money was to be made available for the purchase of the newspaper. It was agreed in a deposit agreement that the money from the South African Government should go to Thesaurus Continental Securities Corporation (hereinafter referred to as Thesaurus), a subsidiary of the Union Bank of Switzerland, and through Thesaurus to the Star Newspaper Comapny for the newspaper and the shares.

10.15 As far as the Commission could establish, two agreements were concluded on the same day. One of these is contained in Exhibit 36E handed in to the Commission by Mr. Kemp. This refers to the making available of money for the purchase of 1,000 shares in the Star Newspaper Company at $1,000 each. The other agreement, hereinafter referred to as the "deposit agreement" (which was not before the Commission), dealt, it is thought, with the making available of $10,000,000 by the RSA.

10.16 According to the deposit agreement, the principal (the Government of the RSA) instructed the agent (Thesaurus) to transfer a sum of $10,000,000 in the name of the agent "but for the account and at the risk of the principal" to the Star Newspaper Company, Wilmington, Delaware. Later on 30 September 1976, the name of the Star Newspaper Company was changed to Global Communications, and the deposit agreement was amended accordingly (Exhibit 38C).

10.17 Because the project was so sensitive, however, the idea was to channel the funds from Thesaurus to McGoff in such a way that it would appear to be a legal foreign loan. McGoff therefore obtained what may be described as "an interest-free loan" from Thesaurus for $10 million so that, if it should be required of him, he could furnish proof that he had obtained the "loan" in Switzerland and not from the RSA.

(d) Lack of evidence and clarity.

10.18 There was no irrefutable evidence before the Commission as to whether this was a repayable loan or not. Various views are held on the subject (see 131 and Exhibit 38, p. 3). Whatever the case may be, one would assume in the absence of certainty about the matter that if the purchase of the newspaper were to fall through (as in fact it did) this amount, less the costs incurred in the attempt to purchase it, would have had to be returned to the RSA. The negotiations with McGoff in Montreal in September 1976 also indicate that this was probably the case, otherwise McGoff would not have agreed to what was arranged there.

10.19 A further gap in the evidence that could be obtained concerns the agreement between McGoff and Thesaurus on the conditions on which McGoff obtained the transfer of the money from Thesaurus and the extent to which that agreement, if it was more than a mock agreement, reflected the terms of the agreement between Thesaurus and the Department regarding the purchase of the newspaper. It may be assumed, however, that Dr. Rhoodie and his officials had to keep an eye on matters to ensure that the money was properly safeguarded for the RSA.

(e) The take-over of the *Washington Star* falls through.

10.20 According to De Villiers's evidence, McGoff informed them from time to time during the first six months about the progress made with the take-over of the newspaper. It appeared that a banker from Texas, a certain Joe Aubritton [Albritton], was also interested in the newspaper. However, he did not want to buy only the *Washington Star*, but also the owners' two television stations. The owners were inclined to sell to the banker.

10.21 According to the witness, McGoff alleged that the banker was setting up a monopoly in Washington in contravention of the American law relating to news media, and instituted an action against him with the Federal Communication Commission in Washington to prevent him from achieving his object (116) and purchasing the newspaper together with the television stations. This action was prosecuted with the assistance of a public relations company, Messrs. Hill and Nolton [Knowlton]. It failed, the banker bought the newspaper, and McGoff had to pay the costs.

10.22 McGoff considered the action part of the process of taking over the newspaper, and the costs of the public relations company and the case were therefore met from the $10 million (117).

(f) McGoff buys the *Sacramento Union* as a result of a verbal agreement with Dr. Rhoodie.

John McGoff and the *Washington Star*

10.23 About a year after it had been decided to buy the *Washington Star,* and while McGoff was waiting for the outcome of his application for an interdict against Joe Aubritton [Albritton], he and his legal adviser, Jones, visited Dr. Rhoodie in the Republic.

10.24 At a meeting in the RSA McGoff mooted the possibility of using the interest on the $10 million and a part of the capital to buy another newspaper, viz the *Sacramento Union,* in the capital of California. The purchase price for the *Sacramento Union* was $6 million.

10.25 According to De Villiers, Dr. Rhoodie agreed to this proposal, but later, during a further visit to the RSA by McGoff, denied that he had given McGoff the right to use part of the capital amount for that purpose. He did not, however, deny the agreement to buy the *Sacramento Union* using the interest on the capital. The interest on the $10 million came to about 500,000 dollar[s] a year (122).

10.26 When Dr. Rhoodie learned during McGoff's later visit that McGoff had put six million of the 10 million dollars into the *Sacramento Union,* he was upset and said that he would have to obtain Dr. Mulder's sanction.

10.27 De Villiers testified further that he, Dr. Mulder, Dr. Rhoodie, McGoff and Jones later had discussions on the matter in Montreal on about 30 September 1976. Dr. Rhoodie again made the point that he had never given McGoff approval for the six million dollars or any part of the capital amount of 10 million dollars to be used for the purchase of the *Sacramento Union.* McGoff thereupon revealed that he had already bought the *Sacramento Union* and that the entire balance of the 10 million dollars had then been invested in the running (125) of the *Sacramento Union.*

(g) Purchase of United Press International and Television Network.

10.28 In the meantime a further amount of $1,350,000 had also been made available to McGoff through Thesaurus to buy a controlling share in United Press International and Television Network, hereinafter referred to as UPITV (153) (see Exhibit 38D).

10.29 United Press International held a 25 per cent share.

Independent Television Network (I.T.N.) in London a 25 per cent share, and Paramount Films a 50 per cent share in the UPITV company. According to the evidence, the agency serves about 110 countries in the world with news items and peddles, to put it that way, television news material.

10.30 McGoff purchased Paramount Films' 50 per cent share in UPITV on behalf of the RSA, but acquired it for himself. In connection with the amount of $1,350,000 owed to the RSA he is reported to have said to De Villiers (in De Villiers's words): ["Man, but I understand indeed that I am your representative in that company." (155).]

10.31 At any rate, the $1,350,000 was added to the $10,000,000, so that McGoff had received $11,350,000 from the RSA (Exhibit 38D 12).

(h) The money had to be returned.

10.32 According to De Villiers, McGoff's actions did not meet with the approval of Dr. Mulder and Dr. Rhoodie, and at the meeting in Montreal it was said that McGoff should sell the *Sacramento Union* and repay the money. He said that McGoff argued that it could not be done immediately, and asked to be given time to repay the money.

10.33 It was then agreed among them verbally that McGoff should pay over the entire profit of the newspaper to Thesaurus on a monthly basis, i.e. about $240,000 a year. According to Reynders's report (Exhibit 38F) to Genl Van den Bergh, there were no profits. A total of $380,000 was at any rate repaid to Thesaurus, and there was $10,970,000 still owing out of the total of $10,000,000 plus the $1,350,000 used to obtain the controlling share in UPITV.

10.34 Several months after the agreement had been reached on 30 September 1976, it was felt that the money was being repaid too slowly. Dr. Rhoodie needed money for other projects, e.g. Annemarie. McGoff, in turn, was involved in a lawsuit which required him to give a full statement of his assets and liabilities. The existence of a foreign loan such as the one with Thesaurus would destroy him politically if it became known. He therefore wanted to sever his financial ties with the RSA.

10.35 McGoff and Dr. Rhoodie then agreed that the former

would repay a further $4,570,000 in cash at that stage. A total of $4,970,000 was therefore repaid and Dr. Rhoodie and McGoff further agreed, without Treasury approval, to reduce the balance of the loan to $1,000,000, that is, according to De Villiers, $5,380,000 of the debt was written off.

10.36 In March 1978 this debt of $1,000,000 was sold to McGoff's partner, one Leipprandt, for $30,000 under a further agreement (Exhibit 38A).

B. *Dr. Mulder Refuses to Give Evidence*

10.37 Dr. Mulder, the former Minister of Information, was subpoenaed to give evidence before the Commission in connection with the *Star* project and the printing of the periodical *Panorama*. He refused to give evidence, and the Commission has referred him to the Attorney-General of the Transvaal for prosecution on a charge of contempt of the Commission.

10.38 According to newspaper reports, Dr. Mulder contended that he had refused to give evidence because the Commission had refused to give him a fair hearing by not giving him access to files. Later, after he had refused to give evidence, he stated, according to press reports, that the Commission had shifted its position by saying that it would make the documents available to him after he had taken the oath. Both statements are untrue, and a true record of the events is given below.

10.39 Before the Commission commenced its session on the morning of 26 April 1979, when Dr. Mulder was to have given evidence in terms of the subpoena, his legal representative submitted Exhibit 60 to the Commission, in which the reasons why he would not give evidence were set out. In this document it is stated clearly: ["After mature reflection and with complete understanding of the consequences, Dr. Mulder has decided that it is not possible for him to testify before you (the Commission) again."]

10.40 Exhibit 60 speaks for itself and need not be discussed in detail except to say that it is not true to the facts. Dr. Mulder had already given evidence before the Commission on two occasions, viz on 8 November 1978 and 27 November 1978 (see minutes, Vols. 12, 13 and 14) and he knew that all documents available to the Commission, which is hearing evidence *in cam-*

Appendix B

era, had been made available to him for his replies as soon as the oath had been administered (see minutes, V 1071, V 111, V 1137, V 1149, V 1154, V 1160, V 1167, V 1170, V 1986, V 1992, etc.). If at any time he had asked for time to consider his replies in connection with such documents while he was giving evidence, the Commission would even have given him the chance to do so. He would then, however, have had to give an undertaking of secrecy.

10.41 In the case under discussion the Commission, by way of exception, made certain documents that had been handed in and on which substantial evidence had not yet been given, available to Dr. Mulder before he was asked to take the oath. He was not, however, allowed to remove them from the building in which the Commission was sitting.

10.42 The Commission's procedure as described in par. 10.40 was in no way changed and there can be no question of the Commission's changing its position in the matter of making documents available to Dr. Mulder, since documents and evidence given before the Commission are kept secret.

10.43 In Exhibit 60 (3) it is alleged that Dr. Mulder "had not had any opportunity to react to contradictory testimony nor has he even any knowledge of the trend or nature of contradictory evidence." This is a lie. The evidence of Reynders, Mr. Vorster's press statement, etc., for example, were put to him in detail. (See Vol. 14, p. V 1160 *et sequor.*) Later Sen. Horwood gave evidence against Dr. Mulder and on 27 November 1978 Dr. Mulder was recalled and Sen. Horwood's evidence was put to him in detail. (See Vol. 23, p. 1986 *et sequor* of the minutes.) In this regard Dr. Mulder was treated just like all the other witnesses, and after he had given evidence before the Commission the first time he said, perfectly satisfied: ["Thank you, Mr. Commissioner. Thank you, gentlemen; and thank you for the friendly spirit in which it was possible to hold this session" (2715 *et sequor*).]

10.44 In Exhibit 60, p. 2, Dr. Mulder also alleges that the Commission did not give him the opportunity to rebut its findings in the interim report. In a press statement, dated 22 March 1979, the Commission invited all persons and bodies who could give evidence on matters covered by its terms of reference for the interim report to come forward. Dr. Mulder ignored this invitation. The Commission assumed that he could give no further evidence on the matters covered by these terms of reference than he had already given before.

10.45 Whatever the case may be, on the morning of 26 April 1979 in the conference room, before Dr. Mulder was called to take the oath, the Chairman explained the whole position to him in detail (2715 *et sequor*).

10.46 (a) The Commission wished to hear Dr. Mulder on the findings it had arrived at about which he (Dr. Mulder) might feel unhappy, since the Commission's activities had not yet been completed.

10.47 (b) The Commission wanted to hear his evidence on the *Star* project, including the *Sacramento Union,* and the loss sustained by the State in this matter, as well as about his alleged interference in the awarding of the *S.A. Panorama* printing contract by the Tender Board.

10.48 (c) The Commission explained the whole procedure regarding the making available of documents to him and also pointed out that his allegations in Exhibit 60 were incorrect, and then adjourned so that he could reconsider his decision not to give evidence.

10.49 Despite all this, Dr. Mulder's advocate informed the Commission that Dr. Mulder was standing by the objections in Exhibit 60, and Dr. Mulder added to this: ["I have had an experience that I wish never to repeat. Many thanks."]

The Commission is convinced that Dr. Mulder, as a key witness, could have shed light on both matters, but was deliberately refusing to do so, and the Commission is satisfied that it did not commit any procedural irregularity.

10.50 Apart from De Villiers's evidence and the documents handed in to the Commission by Mr. Kemp in connection with the *Star* project, there were no other witnesses who gave evidence before the Commission on this project and on the spending of money in the USA in this connection. Dr. Rhoodie is abroad, and the Commission could not persuade him to give evidence on the matter. Mr. Vorster testified that he could shed no light on the matter.

10.51 The two advocates who led the evidence for the

Commission attempted to obtain evidence on the *Star* project in Zurich from Thesaurus and the Union Bank in Switzerland, but their efforts were fruitless, since neither Thesaurus nor the Union Bank of Switzerland made any information available to them.

10.52 The Commission wishes to place on record that proper arrangements were made by the Commission through its legal advisers for Dr. Rhoodie to give evidence abroad, without having to return to the RSA and run the risk of being arrested. He elected, however, not to avail himself of the opportunity.

10.53 A proper invitation was also extended to McGoff by Advocates Klem and Van Zyl during their visit abroad to give evidence on commission in connection with the *Washington Star* and the *Sacramento Union*. Although McGoff was invited to choose a venue abroad for this purpose himself, he also did not avail himself of the opportunity to give evidence.

C. *The Outcome*

(a) A loss.

10.54 The outcome of the *Star* project was that the Department showed a loss of $6,350,000 on an investment of $11,350,000 (Exhibit 38A), to which must be added—

(i) a further R400,000 paid over to McGoff for the purchase of UPITV which was not included in the Thesaurus loan agreement;

(ii) costs incurred in the process of purchasing or attempting to sell the *Washington Star* and UPITV; and

(iii) administrative expenses charged by Thesaurus which according to calculations amounted to $25,000 per annum.

(b) Findings.

10.55 The Commission finds it incredible—

(i) that officials of the Department could leave so much money in the hands of McGoff without themselves keeping proper and effective control over the spending of the money;

(ii) that Dr. Rhoodie could agree with McGoff verbally, without the approval of a higher authority, to purchase the *Sacramento Union*—a transaction involving upwards of $6,000,000;

(iii) that the arrangements between the parties were made in such a lax and negligent way that there is no proper documentation describing the transactions in legally correct terms, or clearly showing the circumstances in which it was decided to write off funds;

(iv) that no one knows what happened to the $6,350,000 that was lost; and

(v) that McGoff as a shareholder is sitting with the *Sacramento Union* and the UPITV, while there is no clarity as to whether the RSA has any right to these assets.

INDEX

Index

Index

Index

Index

Index

Time, 81, 82
Times (London), 81
Torture of political prisoners. *See* Political prisoners, torture of
To the Point, 23, 26, 43–45
Treunicht, Andries, 34
Triumph Fertilizers (company), 110, 113, 114, 118, 119
Tunney, John, 33
Tutu, Bishop Desmond M., 74, 78, 91–92

UBJ. *See* Union of Black Journalists
Uganda, 90
Union Bank of Switzerland, 138–39, 146
Union of Black Journalists (UBJ), 57, 58, 60–61, 65. *See also* Writers Association of South Africa
Uni Rhodes Mining and Finance Ltd., 11
United Nations: and South Africa, 8, 80; Unit on Apartheid, 63
United party, 70–71
United Press International Television News (UPITN), 26, 141–42, 146, 147
United States, relations with South Africa, 8, 30, 33–34, 73–74, 136–37. *See also* Muldergate
United States Federal Communications Commission, 140
United States International Communications Agency (ICA), 73, 74
UPITN. See United Press International Television News
Utley, Garrick, 88
Uys, Gerhard, 42

Vaas, Beurt Ser, 24
Van den Bergh, Hendrik, 21, 27, 31, 103, 104; role in attempted takeover of South African Associated Newspapers, 105, 106; role in founding and financing of the *Citizen,* 109, 110–11,

116, 119, 123–24, 125–27, 128, 129, 133
Van Rooyen, Retief, 29–30, 103, 115, 116, 117, 121, 122–23, 132, 134
Van Zyl, J. E., 67, 146
Verwoerd, Hendrik F., 13, 80
Voice, 60–61
Volkskas Industriele Bank, 119
Vorster, B[althazer] J[ohannes], 13, 22, 24, 31, 35, 52, 67, 74, 103, 104; and the press, 20, 27, 41–42, 49, 69, 82, 83; knowledge of attempted takeover of *Washington Star,* 137, 138, 144, 145; knowledge of Project Annemarie, 106, 110–11, 115, 116–18, 120–24, 125–35; resignation as prime minister, 3, 32, 34
Vorster cabinet: knowledge of Department of Information activities, 32, 122, 123, 125, 130, 131–32, 135

WASA. *See* Writers Association of South Africa
Washington Post, 83, 85, 137
Washington Star, 20, 26, 101, 136–46
Watergate, 1, 21
Weekend World, 8, 40, 57, 61, 97
West, Norman, 16
"White Tribes of Africa" (BBC documentary), 73
Whites, 3, 5, 9, 11. *See also* Afrikaners; Separate development, Afrikaner and British
Wilson, Lindy, 74–75
Witts, David A., 24
Woods, Donald, 8, 9, 47, 57, 62, 65
World, 8, 15, 18, 40, 57, 58, 61, 97
Writers Association of South Africa (WASA), 65

Younghusband, Peter, 84

Zambia, 90
Zimbabwe, 1
Zwelakhe, Sisulu, 15, 18, 65, 94

157